From the International #1 Best Selling Author

DOGS
still
Know
Best

Two angels guide their
human through grief,
learning & love

Angie Salisbury
with Iris Matos

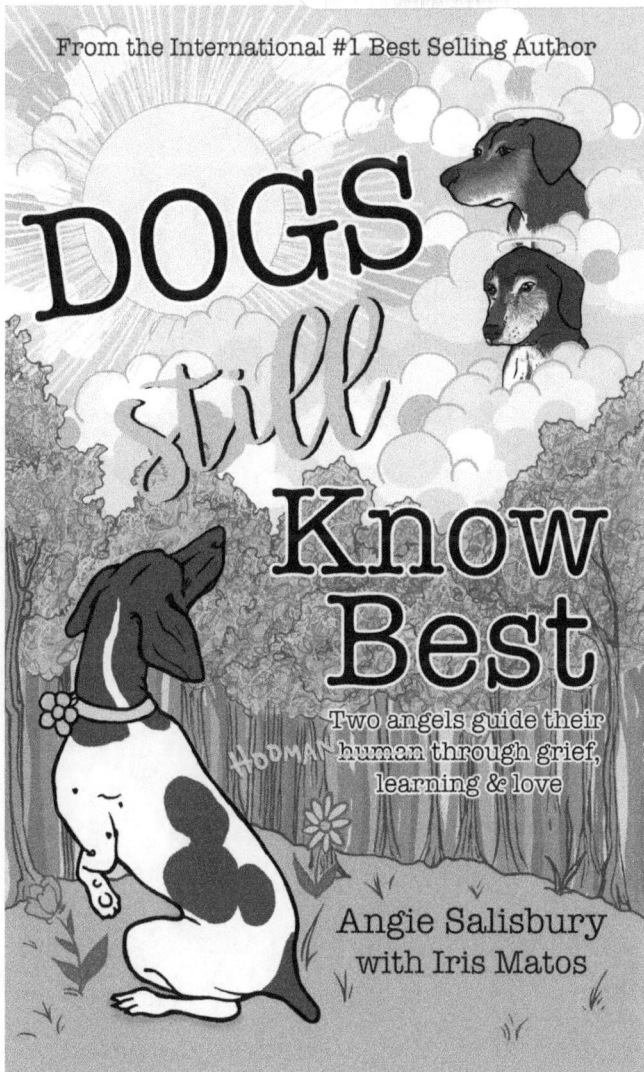

Four Paws Up! For *Dogs Still Know Best*

"Angie is a beautiful, kind soul, and in this book, she does the wonderful service of showing animal lovers how to deepen their communication with their beloved pets, which not only gives more love and support to our furry friends but can spark genuine spiritual growth within us. If you've ever felt that there was more depth in your dog's eyes than you can understand and wished you could connect in a deeper way, read this book."

~Ziad Masri,
Best Selling Author, *Reality Unveiled*

"Truly heartwarming and inspirational! **Dogs Still Know Best** *by Angie Salisbury is a story of love, loss, the long road to healing, and the anti-fragility of the human spirit. But more importantly, it's a story about the impact of enduring*

relationships and the realization that time is all we have - and it's limited. I read this sequel to **Dogs Know Best** *eagerly anticipating the newest escapades of puppies Bimmer and Bertram, only to discover that tragedy had unexpectedly taken these cherished puppies from this world. Instead, this book takes us on a personal journey that would forever change the author's understanding of what IS and what COULD BE as she gains inspiration, clarity, and hope from unexpected companions along the way. Simultaneously heartbreaking and uplifting, Angie's story is a beautiful reminder that we do not travel this road alone; that life is full of both joy and sorrow; and, if we allow it, every experience has the power to mold us into stronger, happier and more empathetic people."*

~ **Jedediah McClure,**
Best Selling Author, *Myths of Christianity: A Five Thousand Year Journey To Find The Son Of God*

"Angie Salisbury puts her heart in the pages of this story and shares her personal journey to strength and happiness. It's a story that is filled with emotion and shares a perspective on life that can help all of us in our own journeys. You'll laugh, you'll cry and in the end there's hope. You won't be able to put this book down once you start!"

~ **Austin Netzley,**
Best Selling Author, *Make Money, Live Wealthy*

Dogs *Still* Know Best

Two Angels Guide Their Human Through Grief, Learning & Love

Angie Salisbury
with Iris Matos

1st Edition
(Book 2 in the Two Dogs' Series)

Annibury
Annibury Publishing

Synopsis

The Pointers are back! This time as two of the sweetest, wisest angels you can imagine.

Much has happened since *Dogs Know Best: Two Dogs' Training Guide For Humans* stole the hearts of dog lovers around the world. There has been a lot of grief, a lot of learning and an infinite amount of love. In this touching sequel, follow Angie's very personal account of how the Pointers sparked her spiritual journey, one that allowed her to open her heart, open her mind and in the process, receive amazing gifts, the biggest one of all being her new love, a sweet little Pointer named Minnie. The result is a dramatic shift in perspective about life, grief and embracing a new way of thinking. And with all three of her beloved Pointers by her side, every step of the journey is filled with love and support. In fact, there's a whole cheering section along for the ride!

On the other side, love is everything.

Dedication

To my angels Bimmer and Bertram,
forever by my side and in my soul.
To Tom, Minnie, my family and friends,
you all hold pieces of my heart.
- Angie

To all the beautiful Shelties who
have filled our home with love,
laughter and barking.
To Jim, you are the best part of my life.
- Iris

What's Inside

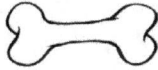

Author's Note

The stories I share in this book are all true – they are direct experiences I have had. If you don't believe in Spirits, Spirit visits, The Rainbow Bridge, life after death and reincarnation, that's cool. I only ask that you keep an open mind. I invite you to enjoy a heart-warming love story about dogs and their relationship with their human, and maybe read a thing or two that makes you pause and consider for your own life. And fair warning, because these are stories brimming with emotion, you're going to encounter the occasional colorful word or phrase.

No matter where or in what direction your own life journey and your beliefs take you, make it your own. Embrace it and live it to the fullest. And above all else, hug your dogs and hold them close, keeping them forever in your heart.

Foreword

Many humans have been fortunate to have experienced living with a beloved dog. Our dogs need us just as much as we need them. This unique relationship that we create with our dogs of living, playing, learning and snuggling with them nourishes both our Souls as well as theirs. Yes, the Earth's animals do have Souls! Of all the animals on this planet, my belief is that dogs have one of the purest forms of a Soul. Dogs provide their "owners" with unconditional love, empathy, companionship and protection. Their love for us, their humans, shines brightly from their beautiful eyes.

Growing up, my family adopted dogs from shelters, and in high school I rescued a dog from the side of the freeway. Just like Angie, I learned life lessons from dogs, especially from my last dog, Riley. My Riley was a bloodhound-lab mix with a strong-willed personality and finicky eating habits. We found each other at a shelter when he was 5 months old. I just knew that he was the right dog for me. Riley came right up to the cage bars, said hello, licked my hand and then lay down. All I heard in my head was a new voice that said "you are my home." I told Riley that I would be right back and marched to the office telling them that Riley was the one that I would adopt.

Riley was quite a handful at 5 months, almost 35 pounds. I learned how to have "recess" again with him as we played and walked in the woods every day. My sweet boy participated in the spiritual classes that I taught to students at our home, and acted as a guardian during Spirit readings with clients. He traveled across multiple states with me as I worked and taught. I appreciated the outdoors more with Riley through our adventures through forests, mountains and caves. Riley was my very own cheerleader during the happy and successful times, and offered comfort and support through the difficult ones. Riley was even excited when he was featured in a couple of magazines and blog articles (he knew this because I talked to him all day long, just like Angie does with Minnie).

One of the most challenging and crushing events that we humans go through is the death of our beloved dog crossing that Rainbow Bridge to Heaven. This raw pain from our dog's passing overwhelms us. The night that Riley passed was a gut-wrenching experience, one I did alone. Being a 135-pound dog and almost 12 years old, Riley's stomach turned and there was only one decision to be made. I lovingly held him close, telling him how much I loved him, how he had assisted me in my spiritual work and how he meant the world to me. He took his last breath in my arms. I bawled for 30 minutes before leaving the emergency vet clinic. For once, I did not have him in the car with me, nor was he there to greet me at the door. The silence was deafening after Riley passed.

As a Psychic Medium, I talked to other people's dogs in Spirit, but that first time I spoke to Riley in his Spirit form was one of the hardest experiences for me. I smelled his unique scent, I heard his voice and then when he materialized in front of me, I started crying. He still visits with me quite often, and helps me in this life as he has done in our multiple shared past lives together.

In *Dogs Still Know Best,* Angie shares her devastation at losing Bertram and Bimmer. The catalytic pain sent her into a search for spiritual truth and guidance. As you read through Angie's guidance and personal stories of these grief lessons, you will discover her *4 Stages of Healing* after the loss of a beloved dog. Her advice provides valuable therapeutic steps that will assist you through the raw pain of loss. When there is much love for our beloved dogs, there will be grief on their passing, as well as hope and joy when you know they are still coming to visit with you from Heaven.

Angie's journey also led her to ministers, friends and finally to my talented friend, Animal Communicator, Iris Matos. Iris provides you with helpful insights on how to communicate with your living pets right now, as well as connecting to them in the Spirit realm. Receive the loving and hopeful energies of this book as you yourself heal. Rejoice with Angie as she introduces you to her new dog, Minnie, and the brand-new lessons that she is experiencing that illuminate that *Dogs Still Know Best.*

Melinda Carver
Psychic Medium, Motivational Speaker
Award-winning Author of *Get Positive Live Positive*

Getting Here …

It was love right from the start
Nose to nose, heart to heart
Forever together our love lives on
I feel you here though you are gone
~ Pet Prayer Flag Mantra

In 2015 I wrote *Dog Know Best: Two Dogs' Training Guide for Humans* as a love letter, a thank you for the wonderful life lessons my two dogs taught me. It was a simple little book in which I chronicled the things I learned from my two beloved German Shorthaired Pointer siblings, Bimmer (a sweet, laid back boy) and Bertram (his girlie, feisty sister). It was a way to remind me and others of the simple things we can do in our everyday lives that will make us happier. I shared the emotional story of our first meeting, coming home together and how they quickly claimed their place in the hearts of me and my husband, Tom. I had a lot of stories to share and lessons learned from our journey together, and in sharing them, hoped that others would learn to appreciate the many things around us for which to be thankful every single day.

Sadly and suddenly at the end of an already-crappy 2016, I lost both of them, just three months and two days apart: Bertram on September 26 and Bimmer on December 28. You can't imagine how grateful I am to have written the book while they were by my side and I could celebrate its success with them; I wrote it for me and for them, but along the way it struck a chord with devoted dog parents around the world.

Little did I know their lessons would continue long after they were gone. But they did and still do. As a result, I embarked on a new journey to do everything I could to open the communication lines with my silly, wise Spirit Angels and learn how to recognize every sign and message they give, me. I do everything I can to live the lessons they came into my life to teach me. And believe me, there are a lot! I also knew they would play a big role in finding the next fuzzball who would come into my life and heart, guiding him or her and me, and helping us navigate our new life together. I knew they would have advice and wisdom to share with both of us, and they haven't let me down yet. Hopefully after reading my story, you'll look at your own dogs a little differently, and be able to recognize any signs that your beloved, departed fur babies are sharing with you.

But let me start at the beginning and catch you up on what's been happening since *Dogs Know Best*.

Bertram (l) and Bimmer (r) waiting to go for a car ride, their favorite thing to do

The Next (Not Final) Chapter After *Dogs Know* Best

Despite being senior dogs (technically considered "geriatric"), at nearly 14 years old, Bimmer and Bertram were full of life and energy. It's true that that energy ran low many days, arthritis was creeping into their joints and naps consumed more of their day, but their minds and eyes were bright and their noses ever-inquisitive. Their ears were beginning to betray them, particularly when in a deep sleep. Tom and I no longer had to carefully tip-toe around them for fear of waking them out of their dreams. Big activity bursts resulted in a much-needed rest day and an anti-inflammatory, as stiffness took hold of their bodies.

The pace of life had slowed but not taken over completely. We spent many hours together sitting on the front steps, watching the world go by and sniffing the breeze. Walks were shorter, and they were happier to stop and lie in the shade or in the cool grass on the hill by the side of the house when we got back home.

But things weren't always calm and serene. There was still a lot of Pointer goofiness in both Bimmer and Bertram, and they were mentally as strong as ever. They loved their squeaky toys and would spend hours on a good bone. Always the chattier of the two, Bertram would "talk" to us all day; even Bimmer got more vocal and more demanding as his hearing started to fade.

As their muzzles and eyebrows turned whiter, our lives were shifting to navigating the world around us with two senior dogs. I became very aware of capturing as much of "them," their essence, as possible – in photos, videos, imprints on my soul. I made it a Point to impress their paw prints in clay, framing them to hang on the wall and using those same impressions to have them engraved into charms I wear around my neck every day, to this day, and tattooed on my shoulder.

I captured the mundane, the silliness, the voice and the uniqueness of each dog.

I wrote *Dogs Know Best: Two Dogs' Training Guide For Humans* as my love letter to them, thanking them for all the richness they brought into my life. I was filling up a memory bank with everything I could think of, trying to prepare myself for a time when they were no longer here with us.

As well-intentioned as that was, nothing can prepare you for that time, no matter how hard you try.

Bimmer's Freak Accident

Ever since Bimmer had his first surgery at 5 years old to repair a torn ACL (the actual surgery was a TPLO – Tibial Plateau Leveling Osteotomy, where a steel plate and screws were inserted into his knee; the second TPLO would come 5 months later, just as he was cleared to return to full, normal activity), we relied on a ramp to get both dogs into and out of my Jeep. The bumper sat high, much too high for Bimmer to manage on his own. Even when he was fully recovered and both dogs were healthy, the ramp helped alleviate any jarring on their shoulder joints that would come with making the leap up or down.

For nearly eight years after that, both dogs patiently waited their turn to get in or out of the car – the ramp was really only wide enough for one of them to use at a time. We had a good system going with never any major incident, until one Saturday afternoon in April of 2016.

We were all coming home from doing errands and both dogs were eager to get out of the car. My husband got the ramp and set it on the bumper like we had done thousands of times before. Rather than waiting her turn, as Bimmer started down the ramp, Bertram tried to get ahead of him. They ended up bumping into each other (okay, Bertram may or may not have pushed Bimmer out of the way), and it didn't end well. Sitting in the driver's seat waiting for everyone to clear out so I could back in the garage, I suddenly heard this blood-curdling scream and howl. I jumped out of the car to see what happened as Tom was bent over, holding Bimmer against his side, his front leg at an unnatural, awkward angle. He got pushed off the ramp and fell off from the full height of the back of the car and landed badly, dislocating a bone in his "wrist."

As Bertram stood close by, Bimmer howled and cried, so with the engine still running, we loaded them both back into the car and rushed him right down to the vet; I called while we were en route to explain what happened and that we were on our way. Thankfully it wasn't even a 10-minute trip. While we waited to be seen, I got a bag of ice from the Dairy Queen next door and we waited in the back of the Jeep, trying to keep him as calm and comfortable as possible.

After a careful examination and a round of x-rays, we were back home and Bimmer's front leg was secured in a splint. We had a choice – he could go in for a very painful surgery with a long recovery time, or we could see how he did with the splint and some time. The overriding factors we considered were that he was an old guy and had serious complications following his latest surgery (he ended up spending the night under observation at the emergency hospital because his blood count dropped throughout the day following surgery). Bimmer had been through so many surgeries in his life – fatty tumor removals, two knee reconstructions and multiple teeth pulled, among others – and the thought of him going through another major, painful one at his age felt like it would have been too much for him.

After a few days, he was getting around slowly. We had a lot of long conversations weighing every angle, pro and con with their beloved, long-time vet, Dr. Douglas Paroff. We decided to hold off on the surgery. Ultimately Bimmer really did great, all things considered. He became quite the celebrity at the vet's office, with the staff regulars greeting him with open arms for his usually twice – sometimes thrice – weekly visits for bandage changes. Soon he was running and bouncing around and thumping like a peg-legged pirate as he walked along, happy as ever. The only difference was he did it with a splint wrapped in really cute designs (a few of which I was able to save), the techs all made sure of that. Whether it was Super Hero logos, Snoopy on top of his doghouse, pumpkins at Halloween, Stewie and Brian from Family Guy (yes, he had very elaborate designs) or countless hearts, Bimmer always was stylin'.

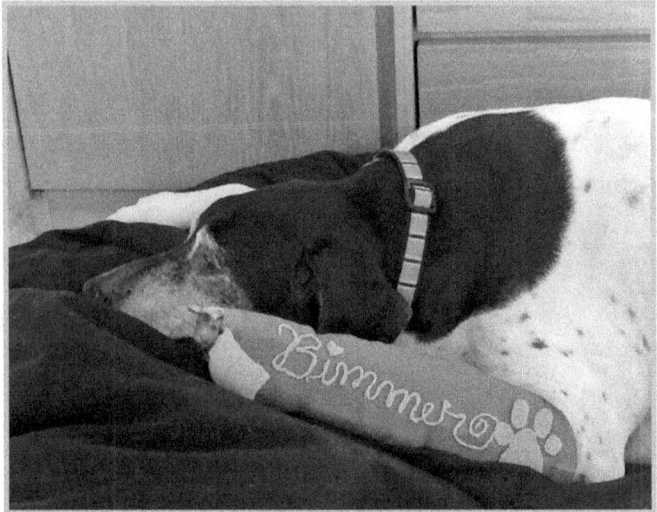

Our daily norm had changed. Bertram still needed her walks and playtime to release her energy. My husband and I would divide and conquer – one of us would take Bertram for a walk or run while the other did something fun with Bimmer. He was always happy to go for a car ride or get some extra yummy treats and attention, then when his sister was back home, he would greet her with a lot of bouncing.

We had a standing early morning appointment time at the vet's. Bimmer was now sleeping downstairs in a decked-out crate/doggie apartment filled with blankets, pillows and toys. It was too much of a risk to have him manage stairs, especially when he was tired. He happily put himself to bed by 7 or 7:30 most nights. Occasionally Bertram would sneak in there for a nap during the day. We did everything in our power to keep both kids as happy and comfortable as possible.

Through all of this, Bimmer never complained. He never growled, he never snapped at Tom, me, Dr. Paroff or any of the techs or staff who were helping him. He maintained his sweet, gentle demeanor, often giving tentative, gentle kisses while getting checked out, staring at us with bright eyes. It amazes me every time I think back; with what he went through, he had every reason to be grumpy and cranky, but not my boy.

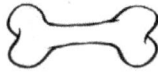

With Love Comes Vulnerability

It was proving to be a rough year. But we weren't the only ones facing challenges or struggling throughout 2016; so many people I talked to had a rough one. For whatever number of reasons, there was a lot of turmoil, hardship, heartache and loss. While I had that general sense throughout much of the year and Bimmer's injury was a constant weight on my mind and heart, I wasn't prepared for the end of September.

My Bimmer and Bertram were closing in on their 14th birthday, so I had been taking conscious steps to celebrate them whenever possible. Writing *Dogs Know Best* was part of that process. I was furiously documenting the mundane, the things that made them silly, those bits of their personality that you can't easily put into words (much as I tried), the things that made them so firmly grounded in my heart.

One Sunday morning, September 25th to be exact, started like any other except for one thing, Bertram wasn't herself. She obviously wasn't feeling well. She wasn't much of a morning girl in general, but there were little signs that let us know something was not right. At this point in their senior lives there were those "off" days, and that's what we hoped we were facing. So, we let her sleep in a bit, then decided to load up the kids for a car ride, always a favorite activity. She immediately claimed her favorite spot in the back of the Jeep, rested her head on the ledge and took a nap. By late afternoon she seemed to perk up and she was more of herself. She had dinner, played for a little and settled in for a peaceful evening nap before going to bed.

We hoped a good night's sleep would do the trick and she'd be back to herself by morning.

The next morning at 4:30, she woke me up to go outside. This wasn't unusual, as she had been in that cycle for several months thanks to her senior girl bladder – she'd cry and wake me and together we'd go downstairs so she could go out. While she was outside, I'd say good morning to Bimmer, who was sleeping comfortably by the back door in the family room in his crate. Sometimes he'd just go back to sleep, other times he'd relocate to their other bed in the room. Once Bertram was back inside, we'd stay with Bimmer rather than going back upstairs to bed, the two of them sleeping while I savored my first cup of coffee.

But that Monday was different. That day, I let her out and she was trotting back and forth along the length of the deck, seemingly uncomfortable. After what seemed like a long time (it was probably five minutes), she came in, then just wanted to go right back out. This happened a couple of more times. She wouldn't settle, and I soon realized something was wrong. When she eventually tried to lay down on her bed, I had to steady her as she got wobbly on her feet. She laid on her bed, never falling into a sleep, and I didn't dare leave the room.

It started as a rainy, gloomy, cold Monday, but was about to get worse.

The alarm was raised; I filled Tom in when he woke up, so we quickly shifted to constant monitoring. Eyes were not taken off of her, looking for the slightest change. I placed a call to bring her to the vet for an emergency visit; something was definitely very wrong.

That visit revealed our worst fears. After an initial examination and x-rays, I had one of the worst conversations I've ever had there. It included the word, "euthanasia." We had one last option, to bring her to the emergency hospital because she was actively bleeding in her abdomen. It was a thread of hope we tried to hang on to. Soon enough, after hugs and gentle words of encouragement from the staff, I was back in the car with her, on the way home to pick up Tom and Bimmer before rushing to the emergency hospital. I called them on the way, so they were ready for us.

Bimmer laid gently next to her the whole way there as she lay on her side, her breathing becoming more labored with each passing mile. I was in tears as I first texted Dr. Paroff to let him know what was happening, and then my family.

We parked right in front of the building and I ran to check in. As I walked back out to the car, Tom already raised the tailgate and was sitting with both dogs. I remember walking up to the car and Bertram looked at me and her ears and eyes perked up, as if to say, "Hi Mom!" It was the most beautiful thing that could have happened – to get that moment of clarity and recognition when she had been virtually unresponsive all day. I have never forgotten that look. Her sweet, bright face is etched in my memory.

We had to say goodbye. A hemangiosarcoma in her spleen (an aggressive, malignant tumor in the blood vessels) had ruptured and she had extensive internal bleeding. She held on just long enough for us to say goodbye before she was gently helped to the Rainbow Bridge.

The three of us – Tom, Bimmer and I – surrounded her and gave her lots of kisses, whispering our I love you's and telling her what a wonderful, special girl she was. I inhaled, capturing her scent in my memory one last time.

It was absolutely devastating and heartbreaking.

By 8:00 that night, we were on our way home, heartbroken, without our little girl. Even as I share this it's like I'm reliving every minute of that horrible day and tears are flowing.

Our beautiful, sweet, bouncy, dainty Girlie was gone.

A rainy Monday ended in a surreal nightmare. Who would have guessed that the absence of one little 62 lb. dog could impact a household so much?

Neither my husband nor I slept a wink, despite being physically and mentally drained. So much stress, so many tears. Sleep would not come, only more tears. The next day I managed to do enough work to accomplish what I had to, then let everyone know I would be offline for a couple of days. In the afternoon, Bimmer had a vet appointment for a bandage change, and I knew that was going to be a difficult visit. We have been going to the same vet since the dogs were puppies, so have come to know the staff and doctors. And since Bimmer's injury, weekly trips (2-3 times a week for many, many months) made us all regulars. News about Bertram spread quickly, which meant a lot of tears and hugs, as one by one, staff members, techs, and doctors came to offer their kind words and sympathy.

We didn't want to go back to a quiet, dogless home while Bimmer was being taken care of, so Tom and I went to a neighboring town to get a cup of coffee and walk around, anything to avoid going home to an empty house. After an appropriately rainy, gloomy Monday, the new day was just beautiful. It was one of those picture-perfect postcard September days – 70°, sunny and gently breezy. It was the kind of day Bertram loved because it meant she could lie in the sun without getting too hot, and catch all the scents that drifted by in the wind as she turned her nose to the breeze. That made me smile; it was truly a day in her honor.

I knew that day was her gift, her way of telling me, "It's okay, Mom. I'm okay."

As it turns out, she was only gone physically. Her spirit was still very much alive, and very much still with me.

I had a new angel by my side.

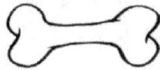

My Sweet Angel Bertram

*"There are no goodbyes because we don't
die, we transform… so see you forever.
See you in the next dimension when
our souls are free."*
~ Unknown

Nothing can prepare you for the loss of a beloved pet. Nothing. The loss cuts deep, at times swift and sudden, other times slow and burning. Often from the very first day they are in our lives, they are an integral part of our families, intertwined in our lives. We share our hearts with them every day. Then when they're gone, we're left with a vast emptiness, a feeling like something is missing. Our world is upended and things just seem "off."

I now had to go through a reluctant change in language, which made me incredibly sad. Saying "he" instead of "they" or simply "Bimmer" instead of "the pups." I struggled with it, and those tiny little words impacted my life and kept the wound raw for a long time to come.

What I wasn't able to see yet was what beauty there was in my grief. It meant that this creature, this soul, had made such a strong, indelible impact on my heart. I was a different person because of her, I was better. My ability to love had expanded, as had my ability to shower kindness and love on another being. I was taught patience, forgiving and the true definition of unconditional love.

For the next four days, in the middle of my deepest grief, I'd hear Bertram cry to wake me from my broken sleep at 4:30am. There was no doubt in my mind it was she, and it was the most comforting sound I could imagine. I'd jump out of bed, tell her good morning (through my tears), ask her how she was and go down to be with my sweet Bimmer.

On the fifth day I had a dream that I was riding with her and a group of other people in a large van; we were going somewhere on a road trip (I never did figure out where). The seats were arranged like airplane seats, with aisles between sets of seats. Bertram was lying at my feet beside me. As more people got on at each "stop" and the van magically expanded, I looked ahead at one point and saw my brother's dog who had passed away about five years prior, laying on the floor. He was staring directly at me as if to say, "I'm with her. She's okay."

*Hearing Bertram's cries on those mornings were examples of clairaudience. **Clairaudience** is the ability to perceive sounds, noise or words that come from the Spirit ethereal world. They exist across the boundaries of time and space.*

I woke up again that morning in tears because that message let me know she wasn't alone. After that she didn't wake me up in the mornings anymore because I finally got the message that my grief had been blocking. Although I still woke up at "our time" for several months after that, it was to be with Bimmer, not because she woke me up.

We were entering another new normal. Since Bimmer came with us when we said goodbye to Bertram (which I *highly* recommend anyone with multiple pets do – bring them along or make sure they are present so they can say goodbye), he was quiet for a few days as he mourned her, but he never searched for her. He was grieving, but probably knew long before we did what was happening, that it was her time to go. As a bonded pair not only in this lifetime but in the Spirit world as I would later learn, I can only imagine the conversations they had as that day came closer.

But soon enough, he embraced being the only dog in the house for the first time in his life, and the sole focus of our attention. He got extra love and attention from Dr. Paroff and the staff during his regular bandage changes. Sometimes he'd have to spend the morning there, and that's when he'd get extra sassy, playfully barking at anyone who dared pass by without stopping to give him some loving, until they came back to him.

And that made him happy.

He was feisty, at times demanding affection and settling into his solo role with grace. I'd often sit with him and cry, sharing moments both special and mundane with him, cherishing every second he was by my side.

Time had reminded me how precious it really was, and I wasn't about to let one minute with him go uncelebrated.

"Did What I Think Just Happened Really Happen?"

In mid-December I had to travel for a couple of days to Cincinnati for a business trip. Close enough to drive, I packed up the Jeep and headed down in the midst of a snow storm. Since it was just me and my thoughts for 3+ hours (and the appropriate road trip snacks), I cried most of the way as I thought of Bertram. Meetings thankfully occupied my mind for the next two days.

Once the client meetings were over, it was time to go back home. I left directly from their office, with the plan to pick up a coffee and snack once I got on the highway. I snaked my way through downtown Cincinnati and once I was about a mile or two down the highway, I took a deep breath and settled in for a long ride with my thoughts as my only companion (or so I thought). I wouldn't have to turn off for about 350 miles.

But then I froze (as much as you can when traveling at highway speeds).

I took another deeeeeeep breath.

And there was no doubt, I was 110% sure… Bertram was with me in the car.

She was there with me! I inhaled her distinct scent (I can't even accurately put into words what that scent was, but there was no mistaking it was her) and burst into happy tears. It was her, it was her. It was as if she was sitting right next to me. There was no question, I spent nearly 14 years inhaling her scent that was all her – never to be confused with Bimmer's.

I knew it wasn't residual odor on their bedding in the back of the Jeep or somehow trapped in the ventilation system; the bedding had been washed many times, the inside thoroughly vacuumed and both the heat and air conditioning had been run for months (living in NE Ohio, sometimes in the same day).

This came on suddenly and it was definitely and positively Bertram.

Through my tears I said, "Hi Girlie!! Thank you for coming with me for a ride!"

I inhaled long and deep, over and over, again committing her scent to memory. I know that she wanted to go for a car ride with her Mom that day. She said hello, and surely curled up in the back and took a nap, as she always did on a long ride.

I was beside myself with excitement. I talked to her, told her how much I love her and how happy I was that she came to visit.

You may have heard of clairvoyance, but what about clairscent? When I smelled Bertram's scent with me in the car, that was an example of clairscent. **Clairscent** *is a form of extra sensory perception sometimes called "psychic smelling," and happens when you receive psychic information through your sense of smell. You smell a person, substance or, in my case, animal that is not in your surroundings. The odor transcends time and space.*

All too soon, I reached the exit where I was planning to get a coffee. I was hesitant, I didn't want to get out of the car, afraid she would leave before I got back. I parked, and as I started to get out of the car I said out loud, again as I did every time I left them in the car, "Wait here, Girlie. I'll be right back, you guard the car." It was probably one of the fastest coffee stops I ever made.

To my delight, she was still there when I got back. I was almost giddy, talking up a storm to her. I called my husband and told him, then I called my sister and shared my news.

I sang to her, I gave her updates on Bimmer and what was happening in the house. After about an hour, her scent slowly dissipated, until I knew her visit had come to an end. I was so grateful that I had the best travel companion I could have possibly imagined for that ride home. It was one of the most amazing things I've ever experienced, and something that I'll never forget. (I recently "scent-sed" Bertram visiting me one morning in mid-September, when we were up early. It was about 5:00 am, and our not-yet-one-year-old puppy, Minnie, was curled up on her bed. I was reading in the chair nearby, and I suddenly noticed Bertram's scent – distinct from even Minnie's. I took a few deep breaths, knew it was her and told her, "Good morning, Sweetie!" She stayed for a while, even after Minnie relocated to my lap, as is our morning ritual. There is no better way to start the day than with my two girls napping with me!)

The next day, I opened up Messenger and reached out to a friend of mine, Jenni Vinecourt, who is a Spiritualist Reverend and Medium. I had to share what happened and see if what I think happened really did happen. Her answer gave me the validation I was hoping for, and brought a level of comfort and peace that I desperately needed:

> *Hi Jenni! I've been curious about something but then I had an experience yesterday that reminded me to ask. Do you have experience with dogs coming back to their humans after they have passed? We lost my girl at the end of September and I know that, for the first four days, she woke me up at our usual time, until I had a dream where I saw my brother's dog (who had passed about five years ago), that was my sign that he was with her and looking out for her and she was okay.*

> *But yesterday I was driving back from Cincinnati and just got on the highway, and got a very strong scent of her - I know it wasn't residue odor in the vents (the heat or AC has been constantly running since we lost her, I've cleaned the inside/vacuumed multiple times and washed their car blankets). It was definitely and distinctly her, and it lingered with me for about an*

hour. To me, she was joining me for the ride home and then curled up in the back to nap, like she always did.

What's your take on that, from just a brief description? Just curious...

Only a few minutes passed until I received my answer.

HI Angie! The simple answer to your question is YES! All kingdoms: animal, plant, human, all exist at all times. We just change forms when we die. Our loved ones are never far from us, as Heaven is not somewhere a gazillion miles away. The next plane of existence is sort of like a parallel universe. It is all right here.

Anyway, your dear four-legged was most assuredly with you on the ride home, as well as in your dream state. I also get the distinct feeling that she is with you more at this time of year to help you cope with some sadness that surrounds this season for you.

Be grateful that you have recognized her presence. Many people feel so much sadness and loss that they tend to block the feelings of love and joy that their deceased loved ones can offer us.

Please let me know if you have other questions. Have a great Holiday and enjoy her as she will be back ---

I'm hearing her tell you that she will be around on the 28th.

Wow! What an amazing response. It's true, I had been extremely sad facing the holidays without her, so to know that she visited me to help was almost more than I could handle!

And that she'd be back?! On the 28th?!

She specified a date. December 28.

I was ready.

No, I wasn't.

Not in the least.

"I'll Be There on Dec. 28th"

Four days after I returned from Cincinnati, on top of his dislocated ankle, Bimmer developed an infection that wasn't responding to antibiotics, so ultimately required surgery. As I shared earlier, he was no stranger to surgery; he had his fair share of them over the years, usually coming through like a trooper.

I was wary because on top of being an older guy, he had that overnight stay at the emergency hospital that

I told you about. After a lot of discussion with Tom and Dr. Paroff, I knew he would be in good hands.

The day before Bimmer's surgery I was very anxious that everything would go well. I just wanted to get that phone call that he was in recovery and doing fine. I pampered him and reassured him that he would be in good hands and back home sleeping on his own bed before he knew it. Dr. Paroff and the rest of the staff were going to give him more love and attention that he could imagine. I told him Bertram would be with him, too.

Throughout the day I asked Bertram, out loud, to please be with Bimmer, watch over him to make sure he's okay and everything goes well. I did it one more time before I went to bed, again making my request out loud.

That night, in the wee hours of the morning I was somewhere between sleep and awake, laying on my side. I turned to look over my shoulder and sitting on the bed next to me, in her best Sphinx-like pose, was my Bertram, looking at me with the brightest, biggest eyes. I remember sleepily saying, "Hi Girlie." She wore an expression that reassured me, "I heard you. I got this, Mom. He'll be fine." I rolled over to give her a hug and could actually feel her short, thick, soft fur before, just like that, she was gone.

> *"Seeing" Bertram that night was an example of **clairvoyance**. I was able to see her with my third eye, in a way that transcended time and space.*

I immediately went back to a restful sleep, which was rare the night before a doggie surgery.

The next morning, when I would usually be a nervous wreck, I was calm as I got both of us ready before heading to the vet's. I knew I had nothing to worry about. Everything was going to go smoothly and Bimmer was going to be fine – Bertram told me so.

And he was. He came through the surgery without any problems or complications, and by afternoon he was home, sleeping off the anesthesia on his own bed. I was still relieved, despite his having a very special guardian angel this time. The next few days passed without much excitement. He and I took it easy while he recovered his strength.

Christmas rolled around and I was an emotional wreck. I'm not a fan of Christmas anyways and usually am ready for January 2 to finally come around, but that year it was especially hard. Not having Bertram with us to celebrate was incredibly difficult because she loved tearing all the wrapping paper and tissue, playing with her new toys and enjoying yummy new treats.

But I wanted to make sure it was extra special for Bimmer. He got his own pile of presents, for once, all for him. It had been a rough time for him, too, so he deserved every bit of celebration. Since he was just over a week out of surgery, I decided to stay home with him while Tom went to visit his family later in the day. Bimmer napped while I putzed around in the afternoon. I fed him his dinner (by now he wanted to be hand fed, and who's going to say no to such a cute old guy?), made mine and then we settled in for the evening, Bimmer sound asleep in his home and me watching him through my tears.

Even though it was just the two of us that Christmas evening, given the circumstances and what had happened over the past few months, I could not have asked for a better way to spend the holiday.

By this time, my curiosity to learn more was burning bright. I knew I had not imagined my visits from Bertram, I knew they were real, and she was there with me. I have always believed in Spirits and the after-life, and I believe our loved ones are looking out for us and don't just disappear when they die. I know we each have our Guardian Angels looking after us, but I was now compelled to learn more. To educate myself and open my mind to a new way of seeing the world and experiences around me.

I went to the best resource I knew, Rev. Jenni. I asked what would be a good starting point for me, and she shared that her next Spirit Communication course was starting soon, but in the meantime, she explained that Spirit was guiding me to any of the works by Brian Weiss, but specifically "Many Lives, Many Masters." I opened up Amazon, ordered the book and immediately started reading. Let me tell you, if I weren't already a believer, I certainly would be after reading his account of the Spirit world.

But more on that later.

Journal Entry, Dec. 28, 2016, 2:32pm: When I journaled the afternoon of Dec. 28, 2016. I had no idea what was still to come that day.

Go Away 2016!!!

2016 brought a lifetime of tears. Too much loss and heartache.

There's been a lot that happened this year that made me smile, even cheer (I'm talking to you, Cavs and Indians). But there has been so much sadness and loss, especially weighing down the back half of the year. It's enough. It's too much. 2016 needs to go away.

Enough with losing beloved animals. Enough with losing amazing talents.

It started with the shooting of a local police dog, and ended with countless other deaths – too many to list. Sandwiched in between were a heartbreaking and scary national election, entirely too much societal unrest and division, the loss of my beloved Girlie. Coco [my sister's dog] *soon followed. Friends lost their dogs.*

There's been a heaviness in 2016 that I haven't experienced before.

I'm becoming more defiant in being true to myself and what I want, and brushing away the cult of celebrity and gathering material things for the sake of gathering. I will celebrate true talent and strength of character, generosity and selflessness.

Life truly is too short, as we've learned over and over again this year. I vow next year to continue down a path where I can find happiness and peace. I will surround myself with people I want to be around, and will do things that make me happy. It's a journey that will require me to continue learning and understanding.

I will honor my passions, namely my dogs, and I will continue to write more.

So fuck you, 2016. You brought too much heartache and pain, unbalanced with too little joy and happiness. 2017, it's all on you to bring back joy, lightness and peace. But no pressure.

Spoiler alert: 2017 came through.

This Is Not Happening Again

In a blink it was December 28th.

Remember, that's the day Bertram specified she'd be with me.

It started out as any other Wednesday. The Christmas season had finally relented and the world was in a holding pattern, waiting for New Year's. I was counting down the days until 2016 was behind us. Since work was slow between the holidays, Tom, Bimmer and I went out and about in the afternoon. I remember the three of us coming home and Bimmer being silly, spunky, bouncing into the house by my side and playfully bumping me in the butt with his nose, as he loved to do.

He was happy and that made me giggle.

The day was winding down, and I started to turn my attention to dinner. Bimmer plopped down on his bed in the family room, a usual spot from which he could keep track of me.

By 5:00, things took a turn. We realized he had become completely non-responsive. He was conscious, but seemingly staring off in the distance, watching somewhere far away.

He was not able to move. We called his name. Louder. We clapped our hands in front of his face as loud as we could. We tried to get him to stand up.

Nothing. No recognition. No movement.

Panic overwhelmed as I grabbed for my phone. I dialed the number for the vet's office I knew by heart, grateful when a friendly, familiar voice answered. She gently listened, immediately understanding my urgency. She knew Bimmer and everything he'd been through, and that we just recently lost Bertram. With concern in her voice, she told me that we could bring him in about twenty-five minutes. Although booked, they would make an opening for him.

Within 20 minutes we had loaded him in the car using his blanket as a stretcher, and we made the 3½ mile drive to the vet.

I remember watching him closely during the not-quite 10-minute drive. I looked him in the eyes and told him it was okay if it was time for him to go; I didn't want him to hang on longer than he should have because of his love for us or if he thought we might not be ready for him to go. I told him Bertram would be there to meet him if he was ready.

I was filled with fear and panic, disbelief that we were making a drive that was eerily similar to one we made just a few months before.

It was a surreal moment.

When we arrived, we pulled up to the back door and Bimmer was carried in for an immediate evaluation. We parked and went to wait inside. Many of the staff who had become our friends came to see why we were there so late (we were almost exclusively morning or afternoon clients), and offered hugs, comfort and support after learning the reason. They took turns coming to sit with us. I texted Dr. Paroff just to let him know what was happening, and little did I know other staff members were doing the same. Even though he was on vacation, he showed the text on his phone to his wife (also a vet at the same hospital) while at the dinner table, and she simply said, "Go."

He arrived within a half hour.

In the meantime, Bimmer was getting x-rays to see what was happening. The pictures revealed a body that was losing an unwinnable fight. His liver and other organs had become misshapen due to tumors and were fighting for space in his chest. He was bleeding internally. Surgery was a longshot.

We had to make the horribly difficult decision to be as unselfish as we could and give him peace. He was surrounded by so much love as we said goodbye – not just us, but doctors and staff. He was a special guy who had love to give to the very end of his time here with us.

It was too sudden; he was gone without any warning.

At 8:00 pm and we were back in the car, just my husband and me. I was holding Bimmer's collar – clutching it, feeling the weight of his tags in my hand – staring at it in disbelief. Tears were streaming down my face as I wept. I was in shock. We sat in silence before he started towards home. 8:00. The exact time we were in the car three months and two days earlier, making the long, quiet drive home without Bertram.

Quiet.

Coming home to a quiet house was painful. The silence that I usually welcomed was deafening. For nearly 14 years there was always some activity thanks to the Pointers. Now there was nothing, just the two of us. Between sobs I posted a goodbye to him on Facebook, letting my friends and family know what happened. Messages and phone calls poured in, including one from Rev. Jenni. She reminded me of something very important:

"Today is the 28th, remember your friend in Spirit said she would be with you on the 28th."

And then it hit me.

Bertram knew.

She knew long before I did why she would be back on the 28th – to provide comfort to me and to be reunited with Bimmer and bring him over the Rainbow Bridge. It was one of the absolute most reassuring things I could have heard right then, to be reminded of the date and her visit.

I eventually slid into bed hours later, tears soaking the pillow, mourning the loss of my second sweet, gentle soul.

We were suddenly a quiet, dog-less house.

Normal Redefined Again

Grief is in two parts.
The first is loss.
The second is the remaking of life.
~ Anne Roiphe

Normal had again redefined itself for me. By this point I wished it would stop doing that.

A week later I had my Bimmer back home. The afternoon I brought him home, I threw myself into my work, distracting myself from the quiet. I had to be by myself, just to be alone with my thoughts. It had been one week since I kissed him and rubbed his soft fur. A week that I never wanted to experience, and never imagined could be so painful. Life was too quiet without them by our side; I missed their energy, their warm fur and their big brown eyes. The bright eyes staring at me when I made salads, or when they knew they got us to do exactly what they wanted us to do.

This one is tough.

The next few days and then weeks passed in a tear-stained, swollen-eyed haze. The house was too still without my sweet, goofy Pointers around. I was in shock, mourning those two souls. Work and sleep escaped me for many, many days, until a new sort of unbalance became my norm.

No matter how old they were, some sort of activity was always happening – playing with their toys, "singing" to us, Bertram doing her laps around each room, methodically sniffing the perimeter, Bimmer keeping watch as the world went by outside. Their energy, by this time more calm than chaotic, had been my grounding force.

No matter what was happening around me, there they were, looking at me with those big, dark eyes, letting me know they were close.

I just wanted to put the year behind me. Too many special dogs left my world over the last half of 2016. Several of my friends lost their dogs. The worst came about a month after losing Bertram. My sister lost her beloved, sweet soul dog, Coco. They were a special pair – companions and a championship team. It was another devastating loss. So, while I was still mourning Bertram, I was trying to offer her comfort and support. And then it was time for us to switch roles again after Bimmer died, and she was comforting me through her fresh grief.

I can't tell you how many phone calls we had where we just cried; unable to speak, we had run out of comforting words to say. Our mantra to each other was, "I'm so, so sorry."

It was never enough, but it was all we had.

I ushered in the New Year with a decisive "Fuck you!" to 2016. I actually yelled it out loud.

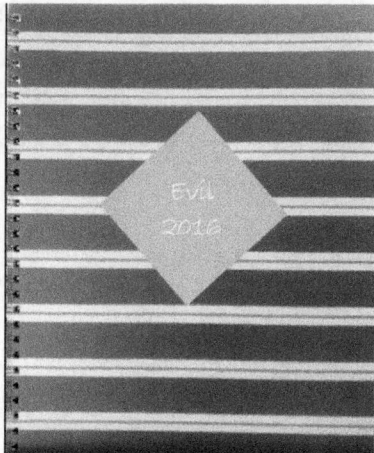

My desk calendar for 2016 is appropriately and forever labeled as, "Evil."

I was angry. I was bitter.

I had too much grief in my heart, too much sadness, too much loss, too much heartache.

Too much of too much.

That year took two of the most important, most valuable and treasured beings in my life away from me, and I'm not sure I'll ever forgive it for that.

Nothing around me seemed to matter. The things that used to feel important were no longer. Knowing that a new year was starting didn't offer much comfort, other than to think, it has to better than the one we just left behind.

Late December and all of January were drowned in tears. The outpouring of love from friends, family and those who knew and loved my kids was a tremendous comfort. My mailboxes – virtual, physical and social – were overflowing with love.

Life came to a temporary standstill, and my heart felt like it was held together with twine and bubble gum.

Sometimes, crying is the only way your eyes speak
When your mouth can't explain how broken your heart is.
~Anonymous

I Needed To Connect

By early January 2017, I again reached out to Rev. Jenni, this time for a full reading. I wanted desperately to connect with both Bimmer and Bertram and make sure they were happy and okay, and that they knew how much I loved them. I knew she was the woman to help make that happen. We scheduled our time together on Friday the 13th. Purely coincidental, good thing I'm not superstitious!

I was nervous and excited, her advice running through my head over and over in the time leading up to our appointment:

"Just keep an open mind. Your loved ones in Spirit already know that we are meeting so they will be ready to go!"

That Friday afternoon, a few minutes before it was time to connect with Jenni over Skype, I sat quietly at my desk. I had already prepared my notebook and carefully selected a pen that I knew wouldn't let me down mid-sentence as I tried to capture any messages I'd receive. I took several deep breaths before signing into the system.

I relaxed as I saw her familiar face appear on the screen and decided to surrender myself into her capable hands and let her guide me through the reading.

Jenni briefly explained to me how our session would go before saying an opening prayer. I took another deep breath. She closed her eyes and was quiet for a moment as I watched the screen intently.

The first loved one to make an appearance was my (German) maternal grandmother, my Oma. Actually, she barged in immediately to say hello and share her love for me, which was very characteristic of her. She was a big personality who always liked to be the center of attention, to be first, and this was no different. Because she (and my grandfather – the entire side of my mother's family, in fact) had lived in Germany and I was here in the States, I didn't get to know her that well, but I know I had a special place in her heart. She wanted to let me know that was proud of me and had a lot of love for me.

Jenni laughed and told me, "I see that you're surrounded by, like, a gazillion dogs and two cats." I've always been a dog lover, it's in my soul. I think the two cats are two that were part of the family as I was growing up. The message from all of them was that they are grateful that I am so involved in and committed to telling their stories. One little white fluffy dog in particular was very connected to me, she explained I knew him when I was little. I'm still trying to figure out who that was!

I knew that writing and sharing stories like this one was what I was meant to do.

As the reading continued, I was astonished by who showed up and I listened intently to the messages or lessons each being had for me. Some were from relatives, some from my guides and animal guides, even the fairies had something to say. But the ones I was most anxious to hear from were the Pointers.

Then, they were up! I was getting to talk to my two sweet fuzzy faces again. And the tears started flowing.

Bimmer and Bertram were indeed together again and were both very happy. They were both feeling good, were no longer in pain – there were no more afflictions, no more injuries, no more arthritis, lumps or bumps. They loved being able to run as far and as fast as they wanted and play.

My heart soared!

Bertram's Soul Mission: A Lesson For Me

Then things got deep.

Bertram came forward first. As I mentioned earlier, we lost her to an aggressive hemangiosarcoma in her

67

spleen. She explained that she *chose* to have cancer, and there was a very specific reason for it. She offered to take that on for me, so that by going through it I would build up my strength. Her Soul's purpose in this lifetime was to teach me strength and courage. So, by her choosing this path, she was helping me grow stronger, to have the courage to face difficult situations. She then thanked me for ending her suffering when we chose to, even though it took us longer to reach that decision than she would have liked. Her words were, "What took you so long?"

I was astonished by her selflessness and love. The thought that she chose that path before she even came into this lifetime was almost too much for me to wrap my head around.

As proof that he was no longer suffering, Bimmer held up his formerly injured leg to show that he was once again whole and he could run and play without pain. He was feeling good.

I wanted to know that we did the right thing for both of by ending their suffering and letting them go. The reassurance I received from both of them was extremely comforting.

Journal entry: *In my dream last night, I don't even remember where specifically I was, but it was a sort of hilly town backdrop. I was walking and talking with someone else, and I remember looking out and seeing dogs running at top speed in two directions. We were on top of a rise, so in front of me and to the left, the ground went downhill then up again and off into the distance. Bimmer and Bertram were both running all out at top speed, then turning around and running back at top speed. It was pure freedom and joy.*

When I woke up, I didn't remember the details of the dream, but I do remember seeing my two with other dogs, running free and fast. No lumps, no dislocated bones. No stiffness, no pain. Just freedom and joy.

That was my sign that they are both together, happy, and feeling good, back in their young, fully grown, muscled and strong bodies.

Strength and Courage

Bertram's teaching me strength and courage was her Soul's purpose in this lifetime, her mission. And part of that lesson for me was to have the strength and courage to let her go when the time came. It was the hardest lesson to learn because I didn't want to learn it. But going through that did help us when it was Bimmer's time.

Bimmer thanked me for not waiting as long as we did with Bertram to let him go, which made me laugh. He clarified that Bertram was the learning curve. He also was quick to add that I should not let those difficult decisions dissuade me from getting another dog and bringing someone new into my heart.

Bimmer and Bertram are together, running and playing. They chose their paths to bolster changes within me, which would result in new, wonderful things for me.

For nearly an hour, I listened, laughed, cried and pondered the messages Jenni delivered from my loved ones and guides. If you've never had a reading done, let me tell you, there is no better way to feel treasured as you not only hear from loved ones, but from ancestors you never knew, from your guides, Spirits, animal guides and many others who are your fans, looking out for you, guiding you and cheering you on from the Spirit world.

Each piece of information was amazing and so special, but at that time, the messages I received from Bimmer and Bertram were the most comforting and the ones I would cherish most. Bertram's lesson ran through my head for weeks, months and longer. It still does.

Her purpose in life was to teach me strength and courage.

I had a renewed approach to my life, knowing I had to do everything I could to honor her and the lesson she was brought into my life to teach me. I owed that to her, and to myself.

My mantra became, "Strength and courage."

I also had to understand that courage comes with pain and discomfort, but as I would learn, that's okay; facing it is part of the growth process.

After the reading my grief didn't magically go away, but I had a new understanding. I had the comfort of knowing the two most important pieces of my Soul were still together. I also knew that I wanted to know more. It was of utmost importance to me to keep finding answers to question after question that kept coming up. To keep learning. To keep exploring this new world, new realm that I wanted to know more about.

This reading would be the first of many for me, and the start of a spiritual journey that would take me places I had never imagined. I wanted to know more as I had new questions for Bimmer and Bertram. I wanted to explore the new possibilities and new gifts. I wanted to learn how to reach out to other dimensions.

My curiosity was sparked. Part of living with strength and courage meant embracing the exploration of new things and new ways of thinking.

"I walk down memory lane
Because I love running into you."

~ Unknown

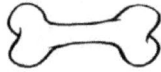

"The Puppy Is Yours"

By late January I was still deep in grief, but I knew there was a lot of room left in my heart for someone else to fill the space. Our house had been too quiet for the past couple of months, and I was starting to get antsy to have another furball running around. I was struggling with feelings of guilt in bringing a new dog home, but I kept remembering what Bimmer said – not to be dissuaded from getting another dog because they were gone.

It started innocently enough by paying more attention to the litters of puppies people were sharing in the Pointer Facebook groups. Then checking out Pointer rescue groups in our part of the country. But there didn't seem to be the right match. I found myself searching in between work projects. I got on the waiting list with our local Pointer rescue group, but weeks went by and I heard nothing.

And then I saw the post. It was Feb. 1, 2017. A man in Central Ohio had a litter of German Shorthaired Pointer puppies who needed homes. He posted pictures of all the pups and their parents and I was inexplicably drawn to them. And they were so close, just down in mid-state! So, I sent him a private message and we started talking. He sent me pictures and described the parents, both of whom were his. He told me about their health and personalities, and a little about their lifestyle. I explained what we just went through and how I was ready to bring someone new home, and I slowly let myself get excited.

But, after talking it over with Tom, he confessed he wasn't ready yet, so ultimately, I had to say no. I was sad and a little frustrated, but I completely understood and respected his feelings. It's a hard thing to do to be ready to open your heart after having it crushed. The puppies' dad from the Facebook group was also understanding.

I wasn't ready to give up.

Several weeks passed and my feelings about getting another dog didn't change; if anything they grew stronger. The topic would creep into our conversations more often, although we both agreed we weren't replacing our Bimmer and Bertram, we were making room in our hearts for another little guy or girl. I again reached out to our local GSP rescue because they had a couple of young adults who needed a home. I finally made a little progress, but the response time was very slow (I later found out they had received a lot of applications for the dogs they had which was great for them, but challenging for us).

Then on the morning of Feb. 24, it was a Friday, I saw the picture on Facebook. The previous evening, the man in Central Ohio with whom I had talked early in the month, posted a picture of a little GSP puppy, perched on his counter, explaining she was the last of the litter who still needed a home.

I saw the post and "casually" (casually meaning I tried not to skip the whole way) went in the other room to tell Tom about her. To my surprise he said, "I saw her picture, too. Why don't you see if she's still available?" I thought my heart was going to explode out of my chest! I squealed in excitement as I ran back into my office to send him a direct message. I was anxious because the post had been up already for about 12 hours, and a lot of people had reacted and commented.

What if I was too late?

I immediately opened Facebook Messenger and contacted the owner, hoping that cutie-girl didn't get a home yet. Here's how that simple conversation went. At that point, not a whole lot needed to be said.

02/24/2017 9:17AM

Hi Keith, I saw your posting that you have one girl still available? Is she still or am I too late to inquire? My husband and I would be ready to bring a new little GSP into our family.

She is still available I had one person inquire about her last night but have not heard back from them yet they said they would contact me today

Ok, I understand. We would be very interested and could pick her up any time this weekend, if that would work for you. We don't want to be GSP-less anymore! Please keep me posted. Thank you!

I will keep you posted as soon as I hear back if not by noon I will message them

Ok awesome, thank you very much. The waiting is killing me! We could get her anytime.

Now I had to wait for what could be hours. I was so excited and anxious that I couldn't focus on anything else but this puppy. I kept looking at her picture, imagining what it would be like to bring her home, what we had to do to get ready for a puppy, and so on. I was pacing, doing anything to busy myself until I heard anything.

Then, just before noon, I heard the *ping* telling me I had a new message.

Four simple words that were about to change my life: "The puppy is yours."

02/24/2017 11:50AM

The puppy is yours

AAAHHHH!!! Yeah!!! Are you going to be around this weekend sometime? We can drive to pick her up.

I was ecstatic! We made arrangements to pick her up first thing Sunday morning, which meant we had a lot to do before then.

Newborn Minnie's first family photo.

Bringing Home Miss Minnie

The next day and a half passed like a kaleidoscope of chaos. Along with inventorying everything we would need for a puppy, we had to get the house ready and buy the things that we didn't have. Saturday evening, I gathered everything that we might possibly need for the 2½ hour car ride home with a puppy, and we finalized when we would head out in the morning. More text messages were exchanged with the owner; I learned that his daughters had named the puppy

Minnie because of the mouse ear markings she had. And when he sent me the picture and I saw her spectacular Mickey Mouse ears, I knew there was no better name for her. It was her destiny.

I was too excited to sleep much, so was up and ready to go early. It was more than just puppy day. That day marked the 5-month point from when we lost Bertram. I was extremely emotional, vacillating between tears of sadness and tears of joy. It was a muddy mix of guilt and excitement.

While Tom showered, I loaded the car and was doing a last-minute check of everything we needed.

In those quiet moments while I was waiting, I stopped long enough to talk to Bimmer and Bertram. We have their remains on a table, and on top of each beautifully carved box is a little custom clay angel statue of each dog. I told them how much I loved and missed them, and that we were on the way to bring home a little girl. I knew they'd like her, and knew they would be with us the whole time.

I gently touched a little Pointer angel ornament that was hanging from the light fixture over the table; I caressed her wings. Little did I know what a significant action that would be. I had bought it before Christmas for Bertram because it was almost all brown like her, and had big wings and a halo. That little ornament represented Bertram, and by touching her wings, I felt like I was reaching out to touch her. As I heard Tom coming downstairs, I tenderly kissed both little statues and one more time said, "I love you guys!"

Then we hit the road. The next several hours were a whirlwind. When we got to the house and walked in, two feisty little puppies and their mom greeted us at the door and a smile came over my face that didn't leave for days. We played with the dogs, and met Caly and Ike, Minnie's parents. We got instructions and asked lots of questions. When it was time to leave, I again felt overwhelming guilt, this time for taking an innocent little girl away from everything she had known in her short life – her mom and dad, her family, her siblings, her home. But I also knew she was going to have a wonderful life with us, and we'd do everything we could to make her feel comfortable and loved.

> *I would later learn, during a conversation with Minnie and Iris Matos (whom you'll read more about later), that Minnie had been told – by whom, she did not share – what was going to happen, that we were going to come and get her and bring her to her new home. She was scared just because it was new and different, but she knew what to expect and was ready for whatever came next.*

That Sunday was unusually warm for that time of year in Ohio, and I was holding what amounted to a space heater (if you've ever snuggled a puppy you know the heat they give off), so I took off my vest and rolled it up by my feet, not thinking anything of it. Soon Minnie's cries stopped as she settled in my arms to nap, the excitement too much for such a young soul. Aside from a short pit stop at the halfway point, she slept the whole way home.

Once home, Minnie immediately started to explore her new surroundings. She was brave and bold, not afraid to go anywhere or sniff anything. She showed early glimpses of living up to her future nickname, Hurricane Minnie. Thank goodness we were experienced Pointer parents and knew what to expect, otherwise I'd have really thought I lost my mind.

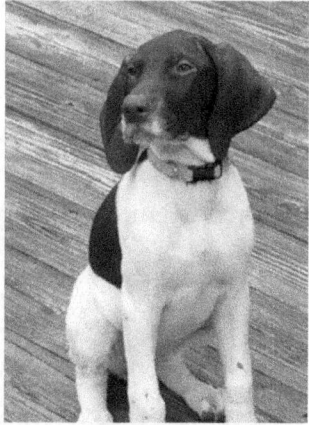

She was everything I was expecting and so much more. While it was natural to compare the things she was doing to how Bimmer and Bertram were, she was definitely her own girl. Bimmer and Bertram were shy when they first came home, not venturing far from the safety and security under the dining room table for about 5 hours, but Minnie boldly explored every room on the first floor and out on the deck. She grew more comfortable and more confident every day, her curiosity driving her nose, and vice versa. And with each passing day, I felt like I was becoming her Mom as we cuddled, played, got to know each other and started navigating our new life together.

I had scheduled a "happy visit" for the coming Friday morning with our vet, really nothing more than a meet and greet. But by Wednesday at lunchtime, we couldn't wait to introduce her to everyone there, so we loaded up for a surprise visit. When I walked in there holding a tiny Minnie, faces lit up. As each staff member came one by one to see and hold her, she was quickly whisked away to meet the staff and doctors in the back. I think it was darn near an hour before she emerged again, this time in the arms of Dr. Paroff.

Minnie and Dr. Paroff meeting for the first time.

We weren't the only ones who were catapulted into her orbit; Minnie had an instant fan club.

(To keep up with Minnie's adventures, follow her on Instagram: @pointtome.)

An Angel in My Pocket

While we were waiting for Minnie to be returned to us, we stood at the front desk talking with the staff and telling them all about our first days with Minnie, and the story of how she came to join our family. Although it was still a mild day, I had worn my down vest – the same one I wore the day we went to bring Minnie home. It was the first time I had it on since

Sunday, when it was unceremoniously balled up at my feet in the car, only to be hung up and forgotten when we got home. As we stood there, I put my hands in my pockets. I realized there was something in my right pocket, which was normally empty (the obligatory wad of Kleenex that followed me everywhere since September was always in my left). Whatever it was, was hard and there were three pieces. I tried to maintain a conversation yet figure out what I had in there. Stumped, I pulled out the objects and instantly froze when I saw what it was. It was my little angel Bertram Pointer ornament, the one whose wings I touched Sunday morning before we left to pick up Minnie. It was in three pieces – the wings, the dog and the base. It wasn't actually broken; it just came apart. In fact, the thin gold wire halo wasn't even bent.

I stared at the pieces in my hand.

Tom looked at me a little puzzled and I showed him what I discovered. I stammered, "I didn't put this in my pocket. How did it get in my pocket?" I think his initial thought was that I absent-mindedly took it off the light fixture, where it was hanging, and put it in my pocket. Maybe to bring it along for extra strength. But I didn't. I was 120% sure I touched the wings, and left it hanging where it was. I would not want put it in my pocket for fear of breaking it.

Knowing it was an emotion-filled day for me, somebody wanted to make sure an angel was with me as we went to get Minnie, and that someone was Bertram. I know she put it in my pocket before we left the house. She was there, telling me it was all going to be alright.

As I stood there holding the pieces, playing with the wings, the dog and the base, my mind was racing. I remembered a fleeting moment on Sunday afternoon, finding the little gold thread that was the ornament hanger, still in a complete loop, on the floor by the light fixture when we got home. I had briefly looked around for the ornament, perplexed. I thought, "I'll have to order another one" since it was so perfect. But since we had a new puppy to fawn over and monitor, I set that thought aside, threw out the now useless ornament hanger and went back to following Minnie around. I didn't think of it again until that Wednesday, as I held it in my hand.

I had just experienced teleportation.

Teleportation: Often seen in science fiction movies or video games, teleportation happens when an object moves from one point to another, seemingly without occupying the physical space between the two points. The object apparently vanishes, only to reappear in a new location. This is one of the ways Spirits communicate with those of us here on the Earth plane.

When we got back home from the vet, I lovingly glued the pieces back together and placed my angel Bertram ornament right where she belonged, on the table with Bertram and Bimmer. And while it started out to be a sweet tribute and reminder of my dear Bertram, it was now elevated to treasured object status.

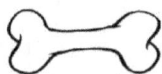

A Spiritual Journey Kicks into High Gear

*"When you are evolving to a higher self,
the road seems lonely but you're
simply shedding the energies
that no longer match the frequency
of your destiny."*
~ Unknown

Thanks to my amazing experiences with Angel Bimmer and Bertram and the other Spirits and guides in my life (Thanks Oma!), I was now on a quest to learn as much as I could about this realm that was so gracefully unfolding before me. I have no doubt this path is the one I was meant to take, and hard as it was, I had to travel this road of grief, strength, trials and courage to get there.

Despite having a beautiful, smart puppy at home, my grief was still strong. Hardly a day went by where I didn't break out into uncontrollable sobbing as I thought of my two angels, often while I was snuggling with Minnie.

Many people who embark on a Spiritual journey do so out of a place of grief or some sort of life-altering event (which can be one and the same), and I was no different. I had now been shown – or rather, led – to a path that would reveal a world I never imagined I'd be an active participant in.

In a dramatic departure from how I was raised, I learned to open my mind and my heart and receive an amazing gift. Those gifts keep coming as I continue to learn, listen and receive. The result has been a dramatic shift in my perspective about life, help in managing grief and encouragement to a new way of thinking.

Question Your Lens:
Growing Up '80s Style

I was raised in an environment where faith and religion were far out on the fringe of daily life. Born to Catholic-Protestant parents, we (my brother, sister and I) were baptized into the Catholic church. We went to Sunday church each week, more out of obligation and formality than actual faith. Case in point, we usually went to the mass that was in Ukrainian because that was a more convenient time than the English service. Mind you, the only one who spoke Ukrainian in the immediate family was my dad, and he'd often skip going to church so he could go to work and then be home with the family in the afternoon. We all knew the Ukrainian version of the mass by heart, and by the time we got to the Our Father on page 86-87 of the booklet, we knew the mass was almost over and it was time to go home. When we reached driving age, attending church was pretty much left up to us. We were C&E'ers for a while (attending mass on Christmas and Easter), but even that quickly faded. The slightest dissent from any of us about going to church could detour the whole thing entirely.

A good part of our upbringing was in the 1980's – the decade of excess – and we lived the embodiment of that upper middle-class excess. Growing up in a big house, wearing designer name brands, country clubs, fancy cars, flashy jewelry, and faraway trips, was, looking back, all seemingly without a lot of substance (which we didn't recognize at the time).

We didn't want for anything. Sure, it was great at the time, but all that came at a price. Actually a lot was missing, as I figured out, decades later.

On top of that, I went to Catholic school. For many, I'm sure it brings them closer to their faith. For me it was the opposite. I learned that there was a lot about the Catholic faith that I either didn't like or didn't agree with, which took me farther away from the Church. That's not to say I don't respect others who have strong faith because I do, no matter what their belief system holds for them. It just wasn't the right fit for me.

Without boring you with a detailed account, let's just say I lived my life. I went to school, made friends, went out, sometimes drank too much, got a job (and another one, and another one...), got a home, got married and found my sweet Pointers. I tried to be as good a person as I could be but wasn't tied to any organized religion. I'd only step into a church for a wedding or funeral, grateful when I didn't burst into flames. I developed my own sort of belief system. I believe in a God, and I believe in life after death, Spirits, the Divine Feminine, Guardian Angels, animal totems, reincarnation, nature, white witches, black magic, voodoo, tarot cards, karma and mojo, all wrapped into one. I believe I am part of a bigger whole, and that I am exactly where I'm meant to be at this moment. I believe that we each have extraordinary abilities to heal, to love, to see, to counsel, to guide and to communicate with and receive guidance from sources not experienced with our five senses.

I can say with 100% certainty that the Spiritual journey that my sweet Bimmer and Bertram started me on came about unexpectedly. But I also am certain they knew exactly what they were doing and setting me up for. I don't believe in coincidences; everything happens for a reason and it happens when, why and where it was meant to happen. I wasn't searching – consciously. I now *do* believe that I was indeed subconsciously searching and ready for this journey and all the glorious experiences it would bring, I just didn't know it. Life's events – good, bad and indifferent – led me directly to this point.

> # What Can Block Spiritual Development
> *Disbelief*
> *Fear*
> *Anxiety*
> *Over-eagerness*
> *Belief System*

I'm thankful they did.

All In

Our True Heritage

The cosmos is filled with precious gems.
I want to offer a handful of them
to you this morning.
Each moment you are alive is a gem,
shining through and containing earth and sky,
water and clouds.

It needs you to breathe gently for the miracles to be displayed.
Suddenly you hear the birds singing, the pines chanting,
see the flowers blooming, the blue sky, the white clouds,
the smile and the marvelous look of your beloved.

You, the richest person on Earth,
who have been going around begging for a living,
stop being the destitute child.
Come back and claim your heritage.

We should enjoy our happiness and offer it to everyone.
Cherish this very moment.
Let go of the stream of distress and embrace
life fully in your arms.

~ Thich Nhat Hanh

After learning a little about my new angels and still pondering the meaning of the messages I received from them, my grandmother and my other guides during my reading with Jenni, I wanted to discover more. I wanted to do everything I could to keep the conversation going and be a more active participant in those conversations. My jumping off point is always books, so that's what I started doing. On Jenni's recommendation, I read Brian Weiss' *Many Lives, Many Masters*. I read Penelope Smith's *Animals in Spirit* and *When Animals Speak*, Tosha Silver's *Change Me Prayers*, Lyn Ragan's *Signs From Pets In The Afterlife* and Ziad Masri's *Reality Unveiled*, for starters. Add to that countless articles and then more books. I began browsing new, different sections of the bookstores, both digital and the occasional physical store, searching for information and direction. I kept reading and learning, opening my mind and my heart to an exciting realm of enlightenment.

One day in April, Rev. Jenni contacted me about an upcoming Spirit Communication class that she was holding, suggesting I might enjoy taking part based on the conversations we've had to that point. I didn't even hesitate because this was my chance to really dive in for 10 weeks and learn as much as I could from a trusted resource, in a safe, non-judgmental environment. I was looking for answers, and I knew that her class would help reveal some of them for me.

The class turned out to be an amazingly enlightening, intimate experience. There were only three of us total (Rev. Jenni, me and one other student), which could not have been more perfect. Each week brought a lot of laughter, a lot of tears and a lot of awe as we uncorked emotions, embraced our guides and explored our intuition. While the concentration was always on the fundamentals of Spirit Communication, each week we practiced the topic that we were focusing on, whether it be cellular perception, tools used in Spirit Communication, receiving messages from Spirits, psychometry and healing, among many others.

I began to understand the synchronicities happening in life around me. I opened myself to signs and symbols brought to me and began to see the world through a different lens, including my grief. I gathered each feather the Pointers left for me, recognized when a Mourning Dove visit was a message from them, and when it was just a local bird passing through. I could tell the difference, I knew it in my soul.

Outside of class during these months, I embraced a regular meditation practice. I obtained my Reiki level 1 and 2 certifications, along with my Animal Reiki certification. I began the path to becoming a Reiki Master.

I could feel myself changing. Growing. Expanding. My awareness sharpened as I shifted my perspective of the world around me. This journey became a priority, something of utmost importance that I was doing for myself. I was trusting my intuition even more than I already did. I truly felt and believed the cliché, "There's more to life than 'things.'" I understood it at my core, it made complete sense.

I began to release clutter – mental, emotional, physical – that had been taking up too much space and energy in my life (and that says a lot because I'm about as far from a physical pack rat as you can get, but a pretty abundant mental pack rat). And it was through the process of release and learning that I was able to ease the constant grief and sense of loss that I had been feeling since losing the Pointers. I could now rejoice and celebrate in the fact that they were with me and, as I'd learn later, with Minnie. I saw the true beauty in their Spirits and in the journey that they took while with me in their physical form. I understood their purpose better, and allowed myself to want to learn even more about them.

When the first class ended and Spirit Communication II was introduced, I didn't hesitate to sign up. The next eight-week session dove deeper into some of the same topics covered in the first class, then moved beyond to more advanced, complex ones like visiting past lives, journeying (a sort of time travel), even trance mediumship. Each week I was learning more and more about my inner strength, my true, authentic self and the natural abilities inside me. This is when I first learned from my guides and Spirits that I am a Healer, a message that would come to me multiple times, from multiple sources.

Field Trip To Lily Dale

No spiritual journey would be complete without a visit to Lily Dale, New York. I'm fortunate to live just a short car ride away, making for a scenic day trip. Located just beyond Chautauqua, Lily Dale Assembly has the distinction of being the birthplace of the Spiritualist movement and a longtime home to free thinkers.

> ***Fun Fact:*** *Lily Dale and the Spiritualist movement in the 1900's served as part of the inspiration for the movie Ghostbusters, starring Dan Aykroyd. In fact, Aykroyd's great grandfather was a Spiritualist and regularly held séances at his home. Learn more about it in his dad, Peter Aykroyd's book, A History of Ghosts.*

Lily Dale can only be described as idyllic. It inspires quiet voices, open ears and open minds. As soon as you pass through the gates to the little community on the lake, you can feel the calm wash over you. It really is like stepping into a different world, a feeling of leaving the modern world behind. It inspires you to put down your phone and just appreciate and absorb the powerful energy that surrounds you. Founded in the late 1800's, Lily Dale remains a community for Spiritualists, Mediums and Free Thinkers. With an impressive array of workshops and seminars held throughout the year, as well as plenty of things to do on the grounds, it truly is a place to discover, to learn and to heal.

That year, we turned the trip to Lily Dale into a sort of class field trip. With only two students and the teacher, the outing was simple to arrange. I was excited to experience everything the community had to offer – wandering along the Fairy Trail nestled in the dense, old growth forest, walking the labyrinth, visiting the pet cemetery, attending a Message Service, going to Inspiration Stump and of course, the Healing Temple. I didn't book an appointment with a resident Medium that day because well, we brought our own who gave us a personal tour.

The thing that sticks out most from that day is the Healing Temple. It's kind of a non-descript little building on the outer edge of the Fairy Trail, right beside the old Lily Dale Fire Company building. Before you even enter, you're greeted by a Prayer Tree covered in thousands of ribbons, on which visitors have written the names of loved ones here or in Spirit, as a remembrance. The messages are tied to the branches, strung together like a glorious garland of love, to blow in the wind and send out to the universe for the Spirits to gather. So naturally, we spent some quiet time choosing our ribbons, writing the special name, and tying them in just the right spot on the tree. We moved inside. A quiet space free of cell phones and really any chit chat, the Healing Temple is a place of reverence and reflection, but more importantly, a place of unconditional love. You feel it the moment you cross over the threshold. In fact, I was so overwhelmed by the indescribable, palpable change in atmosphere when I entered that as soon as I sat down and closed my eyes to quiet myself and do a brief meditation, I started to cry. At first, I thought it would just be a few tears, but the more I tried to control my tears and compose myself, the more I cried, and the harder I cried. This was before the actual healing began. Waiting in the front of the room were about a half dozen Healers, waiting in quiet prayer for attendees to come before them to receive a healing. When it was my turn to take my seat before the Healer, I gathered myself and walked up to her and sat down. She asked my name, and I was barely able to utter something resembling "Angie." She asked what I would like to receive healing for, and it probably came as no surprise, as she handed me a box of Kleenex, that I whispered, "Grief." With the kindest, most gentle smile of understanding, she put her hands on my shoulders and began. It was an overwhelming sensation of solace to be on the receiving end of so much unconditional love and healing white light and energy – no questions, no explanation.

I made my way back to my seat where I tried again to compose myself. Still the tears came. I'm not sure how long I sat there. As soon as I crossed the threshold back into the late summer sunshine, my tears vanished as quickly as they came. I felt lighter, more at peace. I won't say what happened in that building was magic, but it sure felt like it. I was coming out from a darkness, thanks to the light and energy shared with me by my Healer.

That day at Lily Dale was magical, a wonderful way to break away from the outside world. You're cocooned in safety, peace and calm when you're there. I knew I'd be back every year, if only for a day to myself to reflect and meditate in an incredible surrounding, on a beautiful lake in the deep woods of Western New York, to renew my commitment to my Spiritual journey.

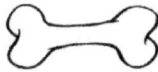

Look For The Signs

Our loved ones in Spirit leave signs that they're with us, and once you shift your thinking and open your eyes, you'll find them all around you. You'll maybe even recognize a pattern of the same sign showing up again and again. Thanks to my own Spiritual journey, I became hyper-aware of any signs from Bimmer and Bertram. How excited was I when I realized that they were all around me? By tuning in and opening up, I allowed those messages and visits to bring me happiness and comfort. They still do, even now, years later.

As you learned in *Dogs Know Best*, Bimmer and Bertram absolutely loved Mourning Doves – sometimes a little too much (yikes, they are a bird hunting breed after all, sorry Dovies)! And the doves seemed to reciprocate, constantly coming to perch on the deck railing or on the ground right in front of the door, despite being under the constant gaze of two bird dogs. So it came as no surprise to me that one of the primary signs they sent to me once they were gone took the form of a Mourning Dove. By this time, I had come to trust my intuition and knew when a dove was visiting on behalf of (mostly) Bertram, and when it was just a dove who happened to be in the neighborhood.

You're probably familiar with the dove as a symbol of peace and love, and probably associate that with white doves floating on ethereal clouds. But I'm talking about a Mourning Dove... grayish, chubby, sweet looking birds who seem to spend more time wandering on the ground as in trees or in the air, and make a sweet, innocent cooing sound. Their penchant for walking around is what got them in trouble with Bimmer and Bertram so often! But in the realm of animal totems, doves represent peace, feminine energy, Mother Earth and creative energy. They are Spirit messengers, communicating between the two worlds. A bird of prophecy, their mournful cooing is often heard most at dawn and dusk, traditionally times when the veil between worlds is at its thinnest point, reminding us that new life is possible and new worlds are opening before us. What an amazing responsibility for such a small, unassuming bird.

At one point in the Fall of 2017, I had a particularly persistent dove who would perch on our deck railing and look directly at me, three or four times throughout the day for four days. If I was in the office, she'd be right outside the window. If I moved to the family room, she moved farther down the railing. Each time I saw her I'd say hello and tell her how beautiful she was, and thank her for visiting. She made me smile. And she kept showing up. Finally, I watched her one day while sitting in my office – at this point she was maybe 8-10 feet away from me – and it dawned on me so I asked her, "Did Bertram send you to say hello to me?" I knew my answer as she stared at me, and I smiled while wiping away a tear. Of course, she did. After that she didn't need be as persistent, her message was delivered. I received confirmation about a month later from my friend Iris, that indeed, Bertram did send that particular dove to me, something I already knew at my soul level (Be patient, more from Iris is coming real soon!).

While Bertram sends me doves, Bimmer leaves me feathers in my path, usually when I'm out and about with Minnie. We can be in the middle of a huge field and I'll look down and there it is – a lone, perfect feather. I find them in random places; on the sidewalk, by the mailbox, out on our deck, often just one white feather directly in my sight-line.

Feathers are messages from our angel loved ones, a sign that they are near, they love you and are doing fine (no, I don't mean when you see a pile of feathers where obviously a hawk or some other predator had a meal. I'm talking about a single feather). I have collected and brought home each feather I find, treasuring them as a little "hello" from my boy. Most recently I had found what I called the "Pointer feather" due to its uncanny brown and white Pointer-like markings in a loose heart shape, the likes of which I've never seen before. That one earned a place of honor in a frame.

My perfect Pointer feather

I noticed something especially amazing about this feather that made it even more special, many months after I lovingly placed it in its frame. One day, Minnie was standing in front of the bookshelf where it rests, checking everything out and bumping a big geode I have on there with her nose (my crystals and geodes are, in her words, "like a beacon to me," and she is continually drawn to them, and will frequently bump them with her nose or try to lick or bite them). Minnie has a distinct white marking on the back of her head, running down the very middle of her dark brown head. As I looked between the back of her head and the feather, I realized the shape of the markings on both is nearly identical. It's like her white marking was reversed and imprinted on the feather. I stared at her, stunned at my realization. That was my confirmation that this feather was intentionally placed in my path, most likely by Bimmer, as a sign that Minnie and I were indeed meant to be together. When I explained my epiphany to Iris and my theory that Bimmer sent it to me, she said, "As soon as you said his name, Bimmer popped in. He said the feather means you're exactly where you're supposed to be." Again, that brought tears to my eyes. And above all else, I knew that Minnie and I were meant to be with each other.

Other signs you can look for may be pennies, rainbows, butterflies, dragonflies, repeating numbers or even hearing certain songs at certain times. The sign may come to you in a dream or even appear in a photo as a shadow or an orb (now *that's* cool!). I've experienced all of these, and I'm thankful that I've opened my mind and my heart enough to recognize them.

At first, I would seek some sort of confirmation for the sign, but after a while, I didn't feel the need to do that, as I knew in my heart and my soul that it was, in fact, a sign from my angels. And trust me, you'll have that same reaction. You'll know when something is a sign, just like I know when a dove is a message for me and when it's just a bird hanging out. For instance, one morning Minnie and I were driving home from the park after playing ball and I turned the corner towards home, looked up and saw a dove sitting on a wire, staring right at us. I instantly knew it was a sign from Bimmer. I didn't even have to think or analyze or guess. I started sobbing; I was overwhelmed with emotion that came out of nowhere, there was no doubt in my mind it was him.

So take my advice. If you think you're being given a sign, trust your intuition and if your intuition says it is, it most certainly is a sign from a loved one, animal or human. Don't doubt yourself, have the kindness and gentleness to allow it into your soul, into your heart.

I've become more aware of my animal spirit guides, and have met many of them through readings and meditation. Each one has come to me for a specific reason, to help me focus on something happening in my life. Spirit animals can come into your life for a specific reason, then leave once their job is done. Others will stay with you throughout your life as one of your master guides or power animals. In order to benefit from their guidance and learn their message, check out one of the absolute best resources, Ted

Andrew's book, *Animal Speak*. It's fascinating when you start to pay attention and understand how each animal totem directly (and sometimes spookily) applies to where you are in your life right now. If you haven't explored this area yet, I'd encourage you to, even if just out of curiosity.

Checking In

"Where there is ruin,
There is hope for a treasure.
~ Rumi

By December 2017, I wanted to have another reading to check in and learn more about Bimmer and Bertram. I had more questions and was eager to find out how they were doing, if they were still together. I was thrilled to find out they were still together and are free of pain and able to run and play as much as they want to. And get this – my maternal grandmother is their protector! Bertram is the social one now, whereas Bimmer likes to hang out with my Oma. So Bertram visits with me a lot, being with me and watching over me. Bimmer visits too, but Bertram tends to "push him out of the way." Bimmer's way around that is to watch over my husband, but that's really his strategy for getting in the house to see me.

This description completely matched their personalities, Bertram was definitely more the social one, whereas Bimmer was happy to sit back and hang out, always a mellow guy since he was a puppy. They told me they are happy when I recognize their signs and messages (to which I high-fived myself for recognizing them).

I learned one of the most important pieces of information about them both – they were Healers. They were Healers for not only Tom and me, but for others that they encountered. They would selflessly take on others' issues and ailments, which ultimately shortened their own lives. In fact, they would have lived longer lives had they not been Healers. When I heard that my eyes welled up with tears as I smiled and nodded my head at learning what amazing, special souls they really are. How lucky was I to have them in my life for as long as I did?

They also had a few words to say about Minnie. Their advice to me with her? Patience. Be patient with her because she is more hard-headed than they were (really? Heaven help me because those two were smart!) and she is super smart. As a result, I'll have my hands full. I need to show her who is the alpha otherwise she'll take over. If I can do that, they said, we'll do just fine. I wish I could say with a puffed-out chest that yes, I am the alpha female, but honestly, I'm not sure any Pointer parent is truly the alpha.

Sigh. And yes, every day I have to work to stay one step ahead of her, and some days I'm not so sure I do!

While Bertram's lesson for me was to teach me strength and courage, Bimmer's lesson for me was love – to teach me about unconditional love. Once again, I shook my head, marveling at how lucky I was to have those sweet souls by my side, both during this lifetime and as my angels. And in those quiet moments when I have a chance to reflect on the world around me, I continue to thank them and honor them by living their lessons for me as best as I possibly can.

I owe them that much… and more.

Dogs Still Know Best

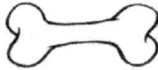

Bimmer Comes For A Snuggle

One night the following April, Minnie was sleeping under the covers next to me as usual. At some point during the night, definitely in the wee hours of the morning, I became aware that the dog next to me was a boy dog, not a girl dog. My intuition was strong, even in my semi-conscious, dream-like state. I also knew that the big brown spots of Minnie's coat, including her trademark mouse ears, were not there. The dog next to me had smaller patches of brown spots. In that moment, I unequivocally knew the dog spooned against my stomach was my Bimmer coming for a cuddle. It only lasted what felt like a moment, but that moment was enough to make my heart sing.

After what seemed like a few minutes, but who knows how long our cuddle actually lasted, I was looking at Minnie standing in front of me on the bed. It was her, but her mouse ears were not there. I reached out and started rubbing her side, and with each stroke, a sliver of her brown mouse ears appeared. I kept rubbing until they were back in their full glory, as if she was reclaiming her body after Bimmer was done.

We both fell into a restful, quiet sleep.

In the morning I clearly remembered everything that happened during the night. While I should have been puzzled and perhaps a little shocked, I was content, happy that I had the snuggle time with Bimmer in his borrowed physical form. I also thanked Minnie for her being so generous to let Bimmer borrow her body (I would find out later from Iris that she and Bimmer made an agreement... he asked her if he could visit, and her response to him was, "Sure!").

Once again, I'm so grateful that I was able to recognize and remember this special moment.

What an amazing gift I received that night.

My Grandmother, My Guide

Perhaps one of the most interesting things I've learned from this journey is that my maternal grandmother is actually one of my main Guides. This explains why she has persistently come forward at any reading I've ever had, starting with that very first one. She was the first one to come forward (remember, she "[barged] forward to make sure she's first." I couldn't think of a more accurate depiction of how she would show herself to me).

My grandmother was a strong, independent, stubborn woman who lived in southern Germany. Those qualities would, at times, put her at odds with my grandfather, himself a proud, regimented (at times rigid) man. In many ways, she was ahead of her time. I didn't know her very well, other than from occasional visits either making the trek to Germany or when she and my grandfather visited us in the States, until age made that an impossibility. Aside from the distance, a language barrier meant any non-visit interactions were pretty much limited to the exchange of gifts and thank you notes. I never had the opportunity to develop a close bond with her, but I always had fun being around her. She was a sharp dresser, always outspoken, liked to be the center of attention, but had a hearty laugh. She was transparent with her emotions, for good or bad. Perhaps one of the things that sticks out most is those rare moments when she would burst into a fit of unguarded, uncontrollable laughter. It always made anyone else in the room with her do the same. We got along well, and she took pleasure in spoiling me. I got to see glimpses of a gentle, softer side that didn't always come out to others. She passed away many, many years ago and while I was sad, until recently I never knew much about her other than brief snippets frozen in the memory of a young girl.

What I've learned recently has forever altered my relationship with her. I now know that she is a protector... not only to my Bimmer and Bertram... but to all animals. She has a deep love of animals, and is a guardian to them all. In fact, Bimmer is happiest just hanging out by her side.

My grandmother was a constant presence during our Spirit Communication classes, even sending messages for me through the other participants to give to me. As I mentioned, she was and clearly still is, persistent.

I'm certain she looked forward to each class, but whether it was to visit me or Rev. Jenni's Dachshund, Rex, I'm not sure. Jenni's two dogs were always part of class, usually asleep and basking in the good energy. During one particular class we were doing an exercise which included a meditation. The room was quiet as we each turned our focus inwards, aside from the light music playing in the background. Suddenly, Rex took a flying leap from his nap spot on the couch and zoomed out of the room – his collar tags getting all our attention, then zoomed back in and back out, back in, back out, until coming back in the room, jumping back on the couch and resuming his nap as if he never left. After the meditation we all laughed and commented on how his "zoomies" came out of nowhere, and went away just as quickly. Well, a few minutes later we found out it wasn't out of nowhere, but my grandmother chose that time to play with him. She explained that while she loves all dogs, she is partial to Dachshunds, and really took a liking to Rex (she probably still visits him!).

Most recently Oma showed up at a Shamanic reading (I told you – every single time!) but this time had a surprise guest, my grandfather. It was the first time he's come forward to me, but I wasn't entirely surprised to "see" him, just pleased. He explained how he is now very different than he was during this lifetime, he is no longer the regimented, rigid man he was, a product of the early 1900's in Germany. He has learned from this lifetime here where I knew him and has changed, now feeling happier and freer because of it.

My Oma is indeed always by my side through the changes in my life along my journey, making sure I don't stray too far from my path. When I do, she gives me a gentle nudge to set me back on course. I know she'll keep popping in. No matter how she's changed, one thing never will… she'll keep making sure she's first in line to reach out to me. And I know my Bimmer and Bertram could not be in better hands.

A Meeting Turns Into A Partnership

Despite everything I've learned so far and my life-changing experiences, I still wanted to know more. I wanted to continue to talk with Bimmer and Bertram, to keep learning about them — their life with me and their life now in Spirit. And now that Minnie was in my life, I had a whole new set of questions to ask and new conversations to have. So in May of 2018, I went to a Spiritual Fair (or Psychic Fair, a place to get a reading from a Psychic or Medium, receive a healing, learn more about your Spiritual journey or buy things like crystals, books, jewelry, decorations and more to support your journey) where I met Iris Matos of Creating Creature Connections, the Animal Communicator and Psychic Medium. I had seen her name around for the past year, but was never able to connect with her. We weren't meant to meet until this point.

Psychic or Medium?
What's the Difference?

Not all Psychics are Mediums, but all Mediums are Psychic. Psychics perceive information using one of the "clairs," coupled with their intuition, even information contained in one's Auric energy. Mediums do the same, but they receive information by connecting to a divine source (loved ones, Spirits, angels, Ascended Masters, guides).

I was excited when I walked in the room and made my way around slowly, saving her as my last stop before leaving; I knew I would have a lot to process afterwards. As I approached her table, she came towards me wearing a huge smile with her hand held out to introduce herself. I instantly liked her. We sat down and I explained that I wanted to connect with Bimmer and Bertram. I brought up pictures of both of them on my phone (out of the thousands of dog pictures on there – I'm one of those who upgraded to a bigger storage capacity phone so I had more room for my dog pictures), and we got right to it.

Iris closed her eyes and opened her connection. Before even a minute passed she laughed and said, "Well, Okay, that was quick!" Bertram popped forward immediately, full of energy and talking very fast, so excited to be connecting. She said she is so happy, she feels great, like a puppy. She loves that she can go anywhere and do anything. She is very active, but is with me all the time. Bimmer came in right behind her, characteristically the more laid back of the two, most likely a sign that he is an older soul. As they were the previous year, they are still together. But now I learned that they are actually a set – they were together before coming to me in this lifetime, they were together with me and they are together again in Spirit. They have not yet reincarnated, explaining they are "in negotiations," which cracked both Iris and I up. I was not surprised by that at all because they were always a team when they were here. Their personalities in Spirit directly match their personalities in this lifetime, Bertram the bouncy, girlie one who was bold and adventurous, and Bimmer the laid back, mellow brother, content to watch the world go by (not to say he didn't have his share of goofiness in him). They are not sad by any means, and do not miss their physical bodies.

Bertram confirmed that she sends me doves, including the one who visited me for those consecutive days the previous Fall, verifying that she left once I realized it was her. Bimmer confirmed that he sends me feathers, and he did come for a snuggle after arranging a deal with Minnie.

Speaking of Minnie, Bimmer and Bertram picked her for me and sent her to me, actually guiding me to her. Bimmer interjected here, telling Iris that I can be "hard-headed, so it took a little extra time for her to get it." That explains the few weeks lapse between when I first saw her and when we actually got her. They said she is very strong – physically, mentally and emotionally – and that's exactly what I needed. They once again emphasized that, while they were smart, she is *very* smart, and she will be a good challenge for me.

Near the end of the reading Iris surprised me by saying they had a question for me. They asked if I was ready for another dog yet. I have to say, I wasn't prepared for that question so it took me a second to respond. I then said I'd leave that up to them since they did such a good job picking out Minnie for me. Bimmer then said to look for a young rescue who will be waiting for me. I know there are three more dogs in my future, and I have no doubt that Bimmer and Bertram will play a big role in choosing each one of them.

Bimmer and Bertram are with me all the time, to them it feels like they are still here. I know they are guiding both me and Minnie, I had yet to learn just how much.

After the reading, Iris and I chatted like a pair of old friends. We discovered we had much in common, it felt like I was talking to someone I had known for years rather than a new acquaintance. She shared pictures of her sweet Shelties; Athens and Siena, then explained how she lost their two predecessors, Snake and Twist, almost on the exact same days as I lost Bimmer and Bertram, in 2015. We both cried happy tears, hugged and made promises of connecting and getting together soon.

I waited the "required" three days before reaching out via email, just like for a date – I didn't want to appear too needy! Her response came almost immediately, and we made plans to get together for dinner. At that dinner, we both proposed business partnerships, and it was then that I knew this was the start of a lovely friendship. For starters, we agreed that I would join her in a couple of upcoming events, and she would contribute to this book.

Minnie Has
A Lot To Say

As part of our collaboration, Iris offered to come to my house for an in-person reading with Minnie. We both agreed that she had a lot to say, and this would provide a foundation to work from.

Let me tell you, Minnie did not let us down! I've included the entire transcript of that first conversation, as well as a subsequent one, at the end of the book so you can read for yourself. Minnie showed a maturity and wisdom beyond her young age, but is still very much aware of her journey. She is being guided by Bimmer and Bertram ("They're around all the time!"), but has not yet "graduated," and has more to learn. Bertram has taken on the role of her mentor. Minnie has a very specific job to do and will do everything possible to make sure she does it. She loves our adventures and takes her work –

barn hunt (essentially hide and go seek for dogs, where they have to find tube with a live rat in it – there can be 1-8 on the course, depending on the skill level – climb on the hay bales and go through a tunnel, all within a certain time limit) and nose work – very seriously.

What came as no surprise to me is she is an Empath. She is very attuned to my feelings and emotions and those of others around her. She has not yet learned how to protect herself from the barrage that she feels, but I know that will come as she grows up. For now, she's "open" all the time, which can overwhelm her.

One of the sweetest things that happened is when Minnie said what we were doing was cool – being able to talk to her. I was extraordinarily happy to know that she wanted to share and have the conversation with me. She asked, "Can Momma do this?" Believe me Sweetie, Momma is working on it! She and I have a strong bond and are a great pair, we understand each other intuitively, and with Iris' guidance, I'm working on going beyond intuition into more direct conversation.

The gift that Iris gave me with this reading was priceless, and I told her so. To be able to have that depth of understanding strengthens your relationship with your dog more than you can imagine. You see the dimension and complexity of that furry soul by your side every day – in my case, every hour of every day – Pointers don't have the nickname Velcro dogs for nothing!

I asked Iris to share more of her insight and experiences here so you have a better understanding of how animal communication works and what kinds of things you can learn from a reading with your beloved pet, either here or in Spirit. And since she lovingly refers to herself as "The Puerto Rican Dr. Doolittle," I had to know more!

.

Iris, The Animal Communicator

Since I love learning people's stories, one of the first things I wanted to know is how Iris became an animal communicator.

How It All Began

I've always been an animal person, it didn't matter what kind of animal. I have just always loved animals, but the path that directly led me here was I lost my mom in 2009. Her passing, just short of her 58th birthday, left a huge hole in my life, and as is the case for many people, I struggled with accepting her loss.

Growing up, we had gone through several religions and none of them really resonated with me anymore, so I didn't really have an output for grief. So I started taking meditation classes, you know, the "gateway drug to spiritual development," as a way to help me cope with my grief. At that time, I had no intention of becoming a psychic or building animal communication skills. I was just looking for a way to attain some peace in my mind and my heart.

As part of deepening my understanding of meditation and the way in which it might help me to gain a stronger connection to the universe, I took a class in psychic development. The instructor and the other people in the class were a lot of fun, and I felt that I had gained so much insight from the experience that I began taking any classes that I could. I mean, if you could imagine a class about spirituality, I took it: Reiki, Tarot, Runes, everything. It was great, for I had a channel for my grief. I learned a lot from a number of talented, insightful teachers, and I found myself developing my psychic abilities on many different levels.

That actually led me to becoming a Pagan because I felt that I already believed a lot of the things in Paganism — nature spirits, communing with and celebrating nature — so that fit really well with me.

I was developing my psychic work, and the more and more I thought about it (saying I'm not exactly the most patient person in the world is an understatement), I was starting to get frustrated with not being able to find my niche.
Knowing that I've always had a proclivity towards animals (my husband used to call me "The Dog Whisperer" because every lost dog seemed to recognize me as someone who'd remove all obstacles to getting them home), I eventually took a class in

animal communication that a friend of mine was hosting in her home. I like to say, "The clouds parted, the sun shone brighter and the angels sang" during that class. I instantly knew that's what I was meant to do in this space. It only took that one class for me to decide that this was the area of psychic study where I felt most at home and could do the most good, for animals and their human partners. It took a little bit, but I know I had to take the path I did to get here.

Since that time, I pursued more intense, structured study and have continued to pursue animal communication through reading, study and experiences of talking to many wonderful animals and their humans.

What Does Being An Animal Communicator Do For You, What Does It Give You?

It fills a void in my life that I can't find in my "real job," my corporate America job in terms of really making a difference in the world. When I was growing up, I always wanted to make a real impact, make a real change in the world. And this is how I do that. It's not a big sweeping change like I imagined, you know, when we're younger how we all think that we can change the world just by stepping out into it. But I can help people who have lost their animals find closure, and help people who are looking to improve their relationship with their animals... really making that change, making that improvement in how they interact. If it's a behavior that needs to be changed that will make their world easier to live in, I'm there to help and that really makes me feel happy; makes me feel whole. That I can make a difference in their lives and the lives of these animals and give them a voice that they may not have otherwise.

Being an animal communicator also filled the void that was left when my mom departed. My mom had such a big heart. She was always helping people and going out of her way to be everyone's friend. I feel like my doing this is allowing me to follow in her footsteps, in a unique way. It is very much a way to honor her. I feel closer to her when I do this work.

How Does Communication With Animals Work?

Do animals just talk to you?

Communication with animals is telepathic, which means I connect to them mind-to-mind and heart-to-heart. The pathway is strongest when I can go through the animal's person, but since that isn't always possible, there are times when I connect directly to the animal, which can be a bit more difficult.

As for "speaking" to me, I am clairaudient, so they can speak to me — it's more like I'm hearing what they are thinking, rather than a specific "voice." While this is fairly direct and easiest to understand, animals will also show me images — a special toy, a friend who is no longer around — that I can understand and interpret. These images are usually accompanied by feelings that are associated with the image, which makes it easier to understand why this particular image is important.

I also feel much of what they feel, and if there is physical pain, they often put it in the corresponding part of my body so that I can relay the information to their person. For instance, if a dog is having some stiffness in a shoulder because of arthritis or an injury, often that shoulder will hurt on my body, and I can let their human know what is going on.

Occasionally, I'll get smells that they are associating with something going on in their lives, but that isn't nearly as common for me as feeling emotions or physical issues.

One story that perfectly illustrates how animals will talk to me involves a dog named Athena. My cousin Wanda is related to me on both sides of my family, so I refer to her as my "Sister-Cousin," and her husband Max calls me his sister-in-law. They have two daughters who call me "Titi (Auntie) Iris," so their American Bulldog Athena calls me that as well. Athena and I have a great relationship, so I regularly get called upon to facilitate conversations.

On one particular occasion I received a call from Wanda who had been trying, unsuccessfully, to bathe Athena. Usually, all Athena had to be told was that it was time for a bath and she would run up the stairs, hop into the tub and wait patiently for Max to come up. This time Athena was having none of it. She simply refused to get anywhere near the tub and fought if anyone tried to force the issue. Wanda called me because she didn't understand what had caused the change ... and Athena was quite filthy at this point.

As I connected, I could feel Athena's relief that I had shown up, and when I asked her about her experience with baths she said, "Titi, the bathtub makes my foot hurt!" I asked her to show me so that I could explain it to my cousin, who promptly made an appointment with the vet. A couple of days later I got text. It turned out that Athena had a small, unnoticeable cut on a pad of one of her back paws. The doctor gave Wanda some salve to apply to the pad to help it heal, and they haven't had any issues with bathing again.

Athena

I do want to mention that some animals simply don't want to communicate with me. That usually isn't the result of anything other than being tired or having something else they'd rather be doing, like eating, playing or working. When that happens, I will respect the animal's wishes and ask if I can try again later. My own dogs, for instance, generally don't want to talk to me when they are tired or hungry, and Heaven forbid I try to communicate with them when they are sleeping!

To learn more about the concepts
of the "clair" senses, visit
http://www.quantumpossibilities.biz/clairs.htm

What Do Pets Think About?

Conventionally, people think animals only care about the basic essentials in life – food, walks, affection. Selfish concerns.

Animals have as full a life as we do, including concerns for themselves, their people and some concern for other people and animals. They think about what their roles are in the family, whether it be as protector, healer, peace maker (like the cat who would sit in front of her people when they were in the midst of an argument) or teacher.

Just like humans, animals have a plan for their lives, lessons they need to learn and a plan for how they'll achieve them. People are always a part of these lessons, in positive and

135

negative ways (for instance, dogs learning to deal with difficult people).

In all cases, their love is unconditional. This love – pure love – is something they express at all times and is something they are trying to teach their people about. We see this and need to accept it as part of why they are with us. When we have difficult pets, that is just a part of how they teach us this lesson. Sometimes they are just assholes, like some people, but usually, it's their attempt to teach us something.

Animals each have very different personalities, just like people do. One time I was doing a reading with a cat who told me to sit up straight because, "it's all about presentation." I've had other cats tell me, "It's all good," like the equivalent of a hippie or a surfer cat. It's funny because people ask me, "Do dogs and cats and snakes have different personalities?" and I have to explain, all animals have different personalities, not necessarily the species. Because while there are some similarities that run through the species, when I'm talking to one dog versus another dog, their personalities can be as different as night and day.

Take the time to listen to and learn from your dog, just like you would with a human in your life. They have good lessons to teach that can make us better people if we are patient and try to understand. Remember, we are a part of their plan for this life just like they are a part of our plan, so we need to accept that and what it can mean for us and our own lives.

It's funny, people will come to me and ask me all these questions about their animals and most of the time they already know the answer, but they don't trust themselves, and they come to me to validate what they already know. And to those people, the people who are really tuned in with their animals I will say, "You don't need me, here are the things you need to do..." I did that with you, [Angie] actually!

What Is The Most Rewarding Part About Communicating With Animals?

You can see the peace that you bring people, particularly with animals that have crossed over. You can see the doubt, the guilt and the wondering if they did the right thing just sort of disappear. I can literally see that energy go out of them; most people are much more peaceful after a session with me than when we get started.

I love seeing the change a reading can bring about in people. When I'm sitting across the table from someone and I'm talking to them, I can see a light bulb go off over their head. They make a connection that they had not made before. You can see it in their body language, you can see it in their face, you can see it in their eyes. Whatever they learned really lightens their load, lightens their outlook and they go out into the world looking at it differently, looking at their relationship with their companion differently. The best example of this is when people have had to make that decision for the last vet visit, and it's always so hard. I mean, I've been through it a lot and that doubt and that guilt and that feeling of, "Did I wait too long? Did I not wait long enough? Was there something else I could have done?" The animal always comes out and says, "It was the right time" or "Yeah, maybe it was a little too long but it was what you needed and I'm here to help you," because it's all about that person. Then having the experience of that closure helps people heal a little bit better and you can see it, you can see the instant when they make that connection or they let go of that guilt or they let go of that grief that is all consuming.

And that's what I love about doing this, it makes me feel happy, like I'm actually doing what I was meant to do. It makes me feel whole, like there's more to me than just going to work at a job so I can pay the bills.

The most startling time for me was the first time I ever sat at a Spiritual Fair and thought, "Okay, I'll do this for you and you can pay me," because being paid was a big hurdle for many of us to get over. That day, a gentleman sat in front of me, and he started talking about his cat that he had just lost a few weeks before. Tears were streaming down his face as I made the connection with his animal companion. His cat, Max, was so loving and so understanding and so supportive of his person, and as I shared this information with him, you could see the man's energy shift. That was the first day of the fair, and literally it was one of my first readings, so it was intense. The next day, he came back and brought his daughter with him to meet me. He got distracted by bright shiny things and wandered off, as is easy to do at Psychic Fairs. His daughter looked at me and said, "Thank you for helping my dad, he has not been himself since Max passed, and last night he slept for the first time for the whole night, he's been calmer..." To me, that was huge. It showed me that I was doing the right thing. It was an intense experience. But, one thing you learn as an animal communicator is that it's not your job to feel that emotion; it's your job to facilitate the conversation. Sometimes it's really hard for me to do that, particularly when I am talking to animals who have been abused. That's where I have the hardest time; that gets me so angry, but you have to stay neutral no matter what the person in front of you tells you.

What Do Animals Have To Say?

Do the animals ever not want to talk about their past and just want to move forward?

Yes. Some will try and help their person understand them if it's actually an issue. My own dog, Athens won't talk about it with me, so I need to call another animal communicator to try to see if they can get him to open up. And then there are times when the animal will say, "Well, that's the past, this person has helped me understand that not all people are like that and I can move forward, so I would prefer to not talk about it."

Are the messages they share mostly positive?

Very much so. Really, their conversation in discussion is mostly about love and their role in teaching us about unconditional love. I've learned that our companion animals' job is to teach us about unconditional love, and even in abusive situations, that animal still loves that person because that's their person. It is hard for me to watch that happen.

How do you handle bad situations and relay that information?

If there is an issue in the relationship between the person and their animal companion, I always lead with love because that is what the animal does. Whatever animal I'm talking to says, "Hey, I want to be a good dog, cat, whatever. I want to make my person happy." And sometimes the expectations of that person aren't what that animal is going to be able to give. But, I'm just the facilitator, I'm an interspecies counselor. It's what I do. So, I help the animal understand better what the expectations are and then I can help the person understand that the animal's capacity for fulfilling those expectations. It may be that there needs to be a compromise in terms of how their life together is approached. And again, that really makes me feel like I'm helping, I'm making a difference in the world. I'm changing the way that these two souls connect. Actually to me, when I'm speaking to the animal and to the person, there really is no difference, I think of them both as people. That's because that's what it is. It's the same energy.

How do you help dogs deal with grief that they are experiencing?

Let's say a dog in this life has lost a companion, maybe it's their sibling, maybe they have lost a cat, their companion. Are you able to help them work through their grief?

Yes, I have been able to do that, and that is more about empathizing with them, understanding how they feel and letting them know that it's okay and natural to feel that way. The most intense example of this was with the passing of my own dogs. For the second time in my life, I lost dogs just months apart. Snake and Twist came to us when they were 2 and 1 years old, respectively. Snake had been there for all of Twist's life and he passed away on September 24, 2015. In June of that year, Twist had gotten a cancerous tumor removed for the second time in his time with us. The first time we caught it quickly enough and he was clear. But the second time it had spread and we knew that Twist wasn't going to be around a lot longer. However, not to be outdone, Snake beat him to the punch by three months. Twist then left us in December, three days after Christmas.

For those three months, it was hard for Twist. Snake had always been there, and without him Twist was having a tough time adjusting. We decided to have a family meeting.

Jim, Twist, and I sat down and had a conversation about Snake being gone and what that meant for all of us. Twist spoke about how his life was so different and how hard it was on him. Even though Snake would still come around to see him, it wasn't the same having that physical presence; it's different than a Spiritual presence. Other animals I have spoken to have said the same thing, "they are still here spiritually and I can still talk to them, but it's just not the same." Talking with my own animals about it is easier, or maybe harder … I don't know actually.

After that conversation, Twist was feeling better about being on his own. It was like being able to verbalize his feelings to us made them easier to handle. He even started to enjoy being an "only dog." The night that Twist left us, I could feel Snake around. One of the dog jobs in our household is to "help" Jim take out the garbage on Sunday nights. Twist went outside as he did every week, walked Jim to the curb, and then laid down in the middle of the yard. He never stood up on his own again. While he was laying there, Snake came and explained to Twist what the process for crossing over was like – he would go to the vet, he would get a needle in his arm and he would go to sleep. And pardon my French, but this is exactly what Twist said, "Fuck that shit, no!" So, while we had planned on taking him to our vet in the morning, he passed away about two hours before the appointment, in his favorite spot in the house and on his own terms. He wouldn't have it any other way.

Helping In Rescue Work

Have you used your gift to help in rescue work? What do you like or not like about doing that type of work?

Working with lost animals is hard. There've been many joyous situations and some really heartbreaking situations… and you never know which one you're getting involved in. Just recently on the heartbreaking side, I had a call from a woman whose cat had been missing for about a week. The very first question I always ask is: "Is the animal safe?" or" Is it still on this side of the veil?" And for the first time in my experience the answer was "no." I had to take a moment to process that because it broke my heart to have to tell someone that information.

Now on the joyous side, the head of the rescue organization that I work with the most called me up and said, "I have a situation. We've tried everything. We know where the dog is, we know he's coming to the feeding stations we have set up. I just can't get him to go inside the trap, so could you talk with him?" The background of this case was that he and his person had been in a car accident. His person was taken to the hospital, and when the firefighter tried to get the dog out of car, he bit him and took off. My heart went out to this woman… her dog was missing, she was hurt from the accident and added to that was she had just recently lost her life partner, who had given her the dog before he passed away.

They knew the dog was in a field populated with coyotes, so we really had to get him out. Since I had so much information (his name, his person's name and generally where he was), I was able to make a connection and get him to talk to me. First thing I could feel was how scared he was. He was shaking with cold and confusion. He asked me, "Does my family miss me?" I said, "Yes, your family misses you. Your mom wants you back. She cries every day." At that moment, I realized that what he was really asking was if his mom was still alive because he didn't know. That was my first conversation with *him. Later that evening, the rescuers asked if I could connect with him again and tell him the plan for the next day. I reached out, but I couldn't find him anywhere. I simply could not locate him. I could not make the connection with him, which is unusual because once I make a connection it is fairly easy to find them again. When I couldn't find him, I was concerned that the coyotes had gotten to him.*

The next morning, I got up and the first thing I did was try to connect with him. Soon enough I found him, but I couldn't get to him. I hit a wall. And what I discovered was that he had a Guide, he had someone who was protecting him, someone who was hiding him at night so that he couldn't be found. As I spoke to this Guide, I discovered it was his dad. His dad was looking out for him and making sure that he was safe. So I metaphorically tuned the radio knob to a different frequency, the one I use for my psychic work. I spoke to the Guide and asked him if he would help get the dog into the trap. I explained to him who we were, what we're trying to do and that this was the best way to get the dog home. And then, all of a sudden, I was able to talk to the dog. I told him that his mom was waiting for him and that this is where he needed to go, this is what he needed to do. I said "Goodbye. Good luck. Take care." At about 3:00 in the afternoon I got a message saying that the dog was home. I felt so much relief that I started crying. When the video of the reunion was posted, my heart was so full of joy that I was able to help bring it about.

Advice On Changing The Relationship

What advice can you give to someone who is looking to change their relationship with their animal companion?

As in any relationship, communication is key. Listening to what your animal companion needs is really the way to change how you relate to each other. It's about building trust, taking the steps to find middle ground where you're both listening to what the other is saying. And you don't necessarily need me or another animal communicator to do that for you. I can help to put words to feelings and needs and things like that, but you know your animal best. You know who they are, and trying to change them can be a lot like trying to change your partner after you're married – it doesn't make sense. Start by approaching the animal as who they are, then work on building your life together.

Input On Family Additions

Just this past weekend, my sister and brother-in-law came to visit with my fur-niece, their dog Bolt, an older Lab. They asked whether Bolt wanted a companion. Bolt was very adamant about saying "Yes, but I don't want it to be a sibling relationship, I want to be a mentor; I want to teach them what I have learned over the past six years." For Bolt, that input of adding to the family was important. You know what? Our animals really appreciate being consulted because they view

145

themselves as part of the family. People say "the pack," but it's really their family.

Athens and Siena

However, animal companions don't always see their person as their parent; they may see their person as their equal, so it's like roommates living together. And, because people generally know their animals pretty well, when I do talk to people whose animal sees them more as an equal rather than a parent, they do not hesitate to agree, "Yeah, absolutely, that's exactly what our relationship is like. I don't call them my baby, they are my companion, my animal, my cat, my dog…" I recently told my husband that it's fitting that our dogs, Athens and Siena, call me "The Lady," not "Mom." Every now and then they will pull out "Momma" when they really, really want something, but for the most part I'm "The Lady." It's fitting for us because we're like two couples living together. Athens was there first, Siena came along after. I brought her in to be his sister, but she has become his girlfriend. It's that kind of a relationship — you can see them get all snarly with each other and then next thing they are making all cuddly.

Are The Messages Always Serious?

No! There's so much fun in their messages. These animals that I've spoken to have such great senses of humor, and a lot of them just enjoy their lives, they enjoy who they're with. Yes, they have a job, but there's so much fun to be had in the world. One of my favorite stories is actually from one of my first professional readings. It was for a turtle, and this turtle was talking about how she enjoyed her environment. Her person asked, "What more can we do to help make her life better?" That's a very basic question that most people come to me with. This turtle was talking about how fantastic her aquarium was, and she was walking me through all the different elements of this aquarium. Apparently, it was enormous. There was this particular outcropping of rock, and what the turtle would do is go up on the rock and kind of throw herself off it, spin around and land in the water below the outcropping. This is her direct quote: "Best thing ever!" That was just a fun, fun reading. A lot of animals will take me through their yard, like if it's a dog and they like to run, they just show me the joy of them running. They like to show me how much fun it is and the joy they have in their lives.

Another one of my favorite readings was with a horse. This horse pulled an image out of my head to help me explain what was going on in his life. His person had asked, "what does he need, what can I give him?" All of a sudden there's an image of the old witch who was the queen in disguise from Snow White, and she's holding out an apple, you know, the way she holds it up to Snow White. I looked at the person and said, "What's with the apples?" The person started laughing. She explained that the horse was getting a little chunky, so they had to cut back on the number of snacks he was getting. He wasn't getting as many apples as he was used to and he was saying, "Bring them back."

One particular conversation that I think fits perfectly here is an on-going one I like to call the "Bush vs. Tree Dilemma." My sister Angie has a Maltese-Shih Tzu mix named Riley, who would come stay with us when my sister was out of town. At the time, we did not have a fenced in yard so we would need to walk him on the leash when it was time to go potty. Though we live in the city, we have about a quarter of an acre of land, and over the years my husband, Jim, has planted various evergreens in the yard. There are a couple of them that never grew to more than about three feet. Riley, not being a tall dog, loved to go over to pee on what he called "the tree." I explained to him that it was actually a bush and that it only seemed like it was a tree because he was a smaller dog. He insisted that was actually a tree and this discussion between us went on for several days. Finally, the day before my sister was to return, Jim took Riley outside for his walk. I'll let Jim finish the story...

"Riley and I always came out the back door and walked clockwise around the house so that he could inspect the perimeter and be sure that no other dogs had been on what he now felt was "his" property.  *That meant walking past a number of trees, shrubs and bushes, many of which were planted by the original owners and were anywhere from 4-feet to 10- or 15-feet high. Riley didn't show any real interest in these and we walked on in silence. I'm not trained as Iris has been to communicate with animals, but I do hear them from time to time. When we got to the back part of the side yard, Riley sniffed at one of the Dwarf Alberta Spruce trees that I had planted two summers before and that was maybe 3-feet tall, and then I heard him, quite clearly, ask, 'What's this?' I was a little surprised to hear him because it is usually only dogs I know well that I can communicate with, so I said, 'What?'"*

"Well, patience isn't exactly Riley's strong point, so he asked again, with considerably more attitude 'What is this?' And he looked at the tree."

"This time I understood, so I said 'Oh, it's a Dwarf Alberta Spruce.'"

*"Well, that wasn't the right answer and his patience with me had really reached its end, so he kind of cocked his head and said, 'No, what is it, a bush? A tree? What **is** it?' as if he normally didn't have to suffer idiots like me."*

'It's a tree, Riley.'
'But Titi (Iris) said it was a bush, not a tree.'
'Well, it is a kind of tree, a spruce.'
'I knew it. It's a tree.' And, he walked with a little more swagger in his gait."

"Because I had no idea that Iris had been telling him it was a bush nor why he wanted to know what it was, this interchange was wholly lost on me until Iris explained that they had been discussing the true nature of the 'tree.'"

During another reading I did for a woman, a dog actually looked at me and said, "Tell her we need to go for more walks because she's getting a little chunky." And I had to say that to the owner, just like that.

So no, messages are not always serious. Our animals have as much of a sense of humor as people do, and I've heard more than my share of proof of that over the years.

"It's Okay To Let Go, I'm Ready"

Are you able to help give a human companion peace when it's time to let their dog go? Letting them know it's okay, they are ready?

That's actually one of the biggest things people come to me about for the first time, when they want to know when is going to be the right time to let them go. I'll connect with their animal and ask, "Okay, what signs will you give them so I can let your person know." I had one dog who actually said to me during a reading, "I'm ready to go now, but I'm hanging on because she [the owner] is not ready yet," and that utterly broke her heart. "I'm ready, I can go any time now, but I know she is not ready for me to go and I'm holding on so she can be ready." You want to talk about tears! Thankfully that reading was done over the phone because I was crying, too. My voice was steady, there was no emotion showing, but I had tears streaming down my face I got a note from the woman several days later saying I took him to the vet and her dog is now at peace.

It's A Sign

What signs their dogs will leave for their humans after they're gone?

They love leaving pebbles by the back door, that's probably the biggest sign I've seen. There have been several animals who have said to me, "Yeah, I left them by the back door," and the owner will say, "Oh yeah! I found that!" I think the reason for the back door is because it's a much more private entrance; it's very rarely at the front door. It might be a rock, pebble, feather or something like a leaf. They leave gifts for their people.

Another sign may be when the person hears their dog's footsteps on the tiles or someplace where you can hear their nails, they love to do that. One dog told me he loved to do that because it freaks his human out, and he thinks that's funny.

Can Anyone Do This?

Can everybody communicate this way with their dog?

Absolutely. Everybody is psychic, everybody has this intuitive gift. I always say, if you are going to run a marathon, you have to train those muscles. It is the same with psychic abilities. You have to learn which techniques and the tools work best for you so you can move forward and for it to become second nature. Start with meditation, the gateway drug. It's really about being quiet, opening your heart and allowing the messages to come in and then trusting that its real; don't doubt yourself.

People do this more than they think, like when you just know something is wrong with your dog and you take him or her to the vet. There is a feeling in your gut telling you something's not right. And, nine times out of ten there is actually something that needs to be addressed. Our animals are really good at letting us know and giving us cues even if we don't "talk to them." It's almost like tuning into a radio station with the old-fashioned radio dial; for example, when I am doing telepathic work, that's one frequency. When I do psychic work, I switch over to another frequency, so it's a perfect analogy. You just have to be tuned in… listen with your heart.

Get A Reading Now!

If you haven't already started looking for Iris on Facebook (Search for Creating Creature Connections) or picked up your smartphone and started dialing her number to schedule a reading for your sweet dog, cat, turtle, horse, parrot, pig, goat or other beloved animal, don't wait. I guarantee you will learn incredible information that will be transformative in your life and in your relationship with your animal companion. If your animal is still with you, don't think you have to wait until they're gone, do it now. The information you learn will be invaluable. And if they have already crossed the Rainbow Bridge, they absolutely will be excited that you reached out and will reassure you they are still by your side.

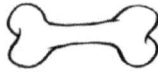

4 Stages of Healing After the Loss of a Beloved Pet

Dogs' lives are too short.
Their only fault, really.
– Agnes Sligh Turnbull

After losing Bertram and Bimmer, I tried to process my emotions, with varying degrees of success. Since it's what I know best and what brings me the most comfort, I turned to writing and tried to compartmentalize my thoughts. I wanted to try and make sense of what I was going through to help others who found themselves in the same situation as me with either a sick dog or one who had more powder on their muzzle than not. I came up with four distinct stages of coping we go through when we lose a beloved dog; they're the stages I experienced for a long time. I know I'll go through them again one day, so hopefully I am wise enough to follow my own advice.

The stages do not have a definitive start and end point, rather a fluidity where one flows into the next along blurred lines. There's also no buzzer that will go off after a set amount of time, indicating that you've spent long enough in one stage and it's time to move on to the next. It's especially important to remember this when we get to the last stage. Life doesn't work that way, and how awful it would be if it did.

Be Gentle With Yourself And Others Will Be, Too

The most important thing to remember when you're going through this experience is to give yourself however long you need in each stage to give your heart and mind time to heal in their own way, at their own pace.

This is not the time to apply logic and ration. This is not the time to scrutinize your reactions or emotions. Just let it happen and be present in the moment when it does. Being mindful of your emotions and feelings will better allow you to process what is going on and give yourself permission to move forward. This is a time to act from a place of unconditional love, the same sort of love that your companion provided to you.

This is a time to be gentle on yourself.

Never feel like you have to explain your emotions. Don't be embarrassed if you get weepy in the checkout line of the grocery store, or while sitting at a traffic light. Don't apologize if a friend says something in conversation that triggers a memory, and tears start to fall out of nowhere, because it will happen. Everyone has experienced some form of loss, so if they have a heart of any size, even Grinch-sized, they will understand what you're going through, offering a kind word, maybe a hug or a gentle touch on your arm. And most times, that will be everything.

On the second day after we said goodbye to our Bertram, my phone rang, and it was a woman who I do contract work with. Thinking I could carry on a calm, tearless conversation about work, I answered it, "Hi Mary Ann."

Always upbeat, she said, "Hi Angie! How are you doing?"

My brave façade crumbled. I was immediately and absolutely overcome. I could barely get out my response, "I'm o----k-----."

I knew I had caught her totally off guard by answering her innocuous question with a sniffling, tearful two-word response, but she gently asked me what happened. I managed to tell her, through hic-cups and sniffles, that we unexpectedly lost our girl. Even though she is not a dog person (rather a... cat person... but I really like her anyways), she offered very kind, supportive words. She explained how she would feel the exact way if anything were to happen to her beloved cat. She encouraged me to take time for my heart to heal, and we'd connect about business later. Her words of understanding brought me some comfort that afternoon, knowing that I was surrounded by people who care.

You'll find kindness and gentleness all around you, sometimes in the most unexpected places. Different people and personalities may express it differently, but the message will be the same.

Stage 1: Preparing Your Mind & Heart... As Much As You Can

When my sweet Pointers got to be around 12 years old, the logical side of me knew I could not take their being with me for granted, that they realistically would not be around for many more years. Throughout their lives, both of my dogs had various health issues. Bertram had a Stage 4 mast cell tumor removed when she was just a couple of years old. Bimmer had two reconstructive surgeries to repair torn ACLs in his knees – five months apart. Both had fatty tumors removed. This was on top of the assorted cuts, stings, allergic reactions, aches, head colds, injuries and other normal active dog stuff. In February 2015, Bimmer had surgery to remove two especially invasive and large fatty tumors. The recovery was difficult and he ended up in the emergency hospital overnight, then back to our vet in the morning. He didn't come home until 36 hours after I dropped him off for surgery. It was a scary time, but he soon regained his strength and made a full recovery.

But in November 2015, there was a different sort of worry. Bimmer again gave us a scare when a specialist discovered a large mass on his liver during an ultrasound. It was one of the first conversations I ever had about realistic life expectancy. Large masses on livers are never good, and the options are somewhat limited with varying degrees of outcome. Thanks to a drastic change in diet, the mass "resolved itself."

While I was elated when I came home to report the results and again when I shared them with our vet, the conversation heightened my understanding of my dogs' age. In my mind, they were still vibrant, active, energetic adult dogs. In reality, they were beginning to experience the difficulties that come with aging, and that required a shift in my thinking.

Honoring them and capturing as much of them in their purest sense became vitally important to me. In the way that made them uniquely Bimmer and uniquely Bertram.

I did this selfishly, for me only.

Lots and Lots of Photos and Videos

I made sure to capture both my dogs in photos and on video, mainly being their cute selves, not really doing anything out of the ordinary, other than being a Pointer. Pictures of them napping, sitting or lying in their trademark positions, certain facial expressions, laying in the sun, watching the world go by on the front steps.

Bertram was our talker. German Shorthaired Pointers are known for being a vocal breed, and Bertram lived up to that reputation. She was constantly "singing" or chatting about one thing or another. Over the years we got very good at interpreting what she was saying. Sometimes it was just to say hi, other times to go outside. There was her "I'm hungry" voice, and her "scratch me, I'm tired" voice. Of course, there was the "shouty bark" when she really wanted to get our attention. With all this conversation, you can be sure I had to capture that on video. And how glad I am that I did.

I can't tell you how many times I've played those videos, smiling at her beautiful voice and remembering her range, and how she talked to us from the time she woke up until the time she went to sleep at night. Or watching Bimmer tear tiny chunks of foam out of a tiny hole in his bed, watching as he intently tore and spit each piece off to the side.

Now it's easier than ever to take ridiculous amounts of pictures and videos thanks to smartphones and tablets. You don't need special equipment, just a reminder to capture the everyday things that makes your dog special to you.

Capture Paw Prints in Clay

I captured both dogs' paw prints in clay while they were still with us. You can pick these molds up online or in many craft stores, you can even make your own. When I got the kits, I prepared the clay and got everything ready... according to the directions, I just needed each dog to calmly stand or sit next to me, hand me their paw as if they were getting a manicure, and allow me to press it into the clay. Clearly the makers of the kit never met a Pointer. After a brief game of chase around the first floor of my house, I resorted to setting the mold on the floor and guiding them both to step onto the mold and... mission accomplished. I've tried that technique with Minnie, but had to give up after five failed attempts. With her, I'll need to wait until she's a little older and is willing to cooperate somewhat.

I carved their name next to each paw print and baked the molds into permanency. I lovingly placed the dried paw print molds into a shadowbox, backed with a black-and-white paw print fabric I bought at the fabric store (check the quilting section for lots of good dog-themed fabrics) and hung it in a place of honor in our living room.

Jewelry

Once you have their paw print in clay, you can have that turned into jewelry. I have both my dogs' prints engraved on a small silver medallion that I wear on a pendant. This is a beautiful, customized way to make sure your dog is with you wherever you go.

I received my charms while both dogs were with me, and now that they are gone, they take on extra meaning. I wear them every day; I've added an angel wing charm between them. I can reach down and hold their paw print in my hand, and I know they are there with me at all times.

Paw Print Tattoos

Admittedly this option is not for everyone, and that's okay. If tattoos are not your thing, just skip this section. But if you have ever considered getting a tattoo, you can have your dog's paw print inked on you. Getting a tattoo while your dog is still with you is a special way to really capture him or her and honor the value they bring to your life. If you know a really talented artist, you can even have their portrait done (but make sure you trust the artist – this can go really bad really quickly!)

I made the decision to have both my kid's paw prints turned into a tattoo about three months before losing Bertram. The decision came on very suddenly, out of the blue; I was compelled to have their paw prints be a permanent part of me. It became one of the most important things I had to do, for reasons I could not explain at the time. My sister called it good intuition, and I think she was right.

The image my tattoo artist (the same artist who designed this book cover!) designed was simple and feminine but beautiful; I was thrilled. When I came home from having it done, both dogs greeted me at the door like they always did (very enthusiastically, as if I'd been gone for two weeks, not two hours). Bertram stood next to me bouncing up and down, her signal that she wanted a closer look. I bent down so that she could sniff and scrutinize my shoulder. I told her that was her paw print. After thorough inspection, she pranced away, satisfied. I knew I had her approval, and I smiled.

Create Memories Together

> *To sit with a dog on a hillside*
> *on a glorious afternoon*
> *is to be back in Eden,*
> *where doing nothing was*
> *not boring — it was peace.*
> ~ Milan Kundera

You've probably seen the stories online of devoted dog parents taking their dogs on a bucket list journey. Sometimes it truly is a grand trip, other times it's a couple of days spent doing all the dog's favorite things. I have to admit, as beautiful as I find these accounts, I rarely reach the end of the story because it's too hard for me. What they're doing is spending "ideal" time together, doing things that the dog loves to do and building memories.

Your time together doesn't need to be grand or extravagant. Your dog wants and deserves to be with you. To have your full attention and go wherever you go; for you to be present with him or her, not staring at your phone or thinking about what you *should* be doing instead.

One of my favorite last memories with Bertram happened about a month before we lost her. It was a beautiful early fall morning, the sun was out, the sky was clear and there was a very soft breeze in the air. We had just dropped Bimmer off at the vet to have his splint changed, so we had about an hour before we picked him up. She and I got in the car, did an errand, picked up a coffee and went back to hang out in the parking lot. Once I parked, I opened the tailgate and she and I just sat. We sat side-by-side watching the world go by in companionable silence. I remember looking over at her at one point and thinking how regal she was laying, so I started taking pictures of her. She was in her perfect Sphinx-pose. My heart warmed even more when she rested her chin on her dainty front paws. She was the perfect photography subject. I remember chuckling to myself, thinking if anyone was watching me from the windows, they'd think I was doing an all-out photo shoot.

Those pictures remind me of a beautiful moment we were together, not doing anything other than waiting, but just enjoying being together.

Journal

A journal is a wonderful way to chronicle the happenings of our lives. Admittedly, I've never been one to journal consistently. Ironic since I'm a writer, huh? I love journal books (and have many on my shelf or in drawers, most still empty) and the idea and therapy of journaling, but I just could never bring myself to do it, until this loss.

One thing I did do, however, is decide to write a book about the life lessons my goofy Pointers taught me. It's one of my favorite things I ever did and the thing I'm most proud of. That of course, is *Dogs Know Best*.

Going through the process of writing the book gave me the opportunity to carefully examine the relationship I had with my dogs, and the impact they made on my life. I made sure their fuzzy faces were on the cover, and I included the perfect pictures to showcase their uniqueness. It was an amazing adventure that I got to share with them every step of the way.

I'm not saying you need to write a book about your dog (but if you do, that's awesome… make sure to send me a copy!). But if you're so inclined, capture on paper or electronically exactly what makes your dog special to you. How do they impact your life? What about their personality is uniquely them? What's that one story you always tell to people you meet that perfectly sums up who they are?

If writing is not your thing, draw a picture. Paint a portrait. Write a song.

Let your mind go and follow your spirit. There's no right, no wrong. No, "it's not going to be good enough." It will be perfect.

A Shift in Mindset

Logic would dictate that, as our dogs grow older, a shift in our mindset is natural and ultimately healthy, easing the transition we'll inevitably have to make. Right. Now when the heart takes over, the conversation changes.

I tried my damnedest to mentally accept my dogs' mortality. I told myself they were getting older, that they both had health issues. I knew that, when we celebrated their upcoming birthday, we may not have many more together.

I reminded myself that when the dreaded time ever came when we would have let them go, it would be when they no longer had a good quality of life or were in pain or were suffering. Because that was the right, kind, humane thing to do. I had to tell myself that we had to not be selfish if we were ever in a position to have to make an end-of-life decision.

I thought I prepared my mind and my heart. But in reality, there's no amount of preparation that you can do. Nothing can duplicate the emotion, the fear, the doubt, the sadness, the guilt, the void, the emptiness that charges in once your beloved dog is no longer by your side.

If you're in the unfortunate situation where your dog is terminally sick or they have an illness that is life threatening, then you may have more time to prepare yourself – to brace for what's to come. You will reach the point where you've done everything you can to help, but it's best to let them go.

With both Bimmer and Bertram, we did not have the luxury of time on our side. Both of their declines were sudden and dramatic, as you learned. We didn't have time to create one last memory, so I'm infinitely glad that I had done the things I did so that their essence and their spirit will be with me always. And thanks to my own intuition and the readings I've had with Iris and other Mediums, I have confirmation of that.

All we can do, as their guardians, is to make sure they are as comfortable as possible at all times, that they are living a good quality of life and we are by their side. Don't turn your back on them just because you may be uncomfortable seeing them succumb to age or illness; that's the time they need you to be with them most of all. They've been with you through good times and bad. They have celebrated your joys and been there when you cried into their fur. They listened to your angry rant about work, and watched as you picked out just the right outfit for that special occasion. Heck, they even made sure nothing happened when you were in the bathroom!

Now it's your turn to be there for them; it's what they deserve.

Stage 2: Loss & Grieving

The act of saying goodbye was one of the hardest, saddest things I've ever had to go through. They were by my side always. Working from home meant many times we were together 24-hours a day. They'd wake me up early to go out, sing or play or bark during conference calls, follow me every time I left the room, come on errands with me. We went to the park together, and on lots of long walks. They slept on the bed and cuddled on the couch while I read.

And then one evening we drove home – just three of us, not four – to a very still house. Three months later, only two returned.

Bertram's young energy was gone. She was responsible for a lot of the noise and activity in the house, which we never really realized until it was not there. She never had the characteristic slowdown of an old dog; she was bouncy, energetic, strong, alert and of course, very talkative. When she was gone, her absence was palpable, and initially, unbearable. That's not to say Bimmer is that quiet of a guy, but he had always been the more laid-back, mellow sibling. We often said that he was quiet because she wouldn't let him get a word in edge-wise! And then his watchful eye was no more.

Our new reality was a much different environment.

Walking in the house was weirdly quiet. There was rarely a time in all the years when we were both home without at least one of the dogs there. But it was just us.

Our new reality made me sad.

Let Your Other Pets Say Goodbye

I remember reading, most likely from an article that showed up in my Facebook feed from one of the many, many dog-related pages that I follow, that if you have other pets in your family, make sure they are with you when you have to say goodbye to your beloved dog.

We did this with our Bimmer, we made sure he was with us when it was time to let Bertram go. When we left the house to go to the emergency hospital, we made sure he came along with us. He waited in the car while we spoke with the doctor. When it was time to be together one final time, my husband went to get him so he could be in the room with us. He sniffed Bertram's face, and patiently waited (although he was a little nervous to be there, he's spent his fair share of time at that hospital). Then we all walked out to the car together.

When we got home, Bimmer soon settled in after getting a drink of water, a little bit of dinner (since he missed his usual dinner time) and going outside. He stuck close by as I made some teary phone calls.

The next two days he was a little quieter than usual, I'm sure partly as he adjusted and partly due to his own grieving and our oppressive moods. But he never went looking for his sister. He never wandered, wondering if she was in the other room. He never cried for her. He knew. I don't know at what level or understand completely how he knew, but he did. He knew she was not coming back, and it seemed that he had enough closure to get back into his routine. Now, a couple of years later, finding out that they are a pair in every dimension, I know that he knew he'd be reunited with her again soon.

When we told our vet that we had Bimmer with us and that he was doing so well he offered, "He probably knew that she was dying long before you did. Dogs have an amazing ability to sense things that we don't; it's not much different than dogs that are trained to sniff out cancer or to sense seizures."

And I believe that 100%, particularly after going through it and witnessing it for myself.

I wholeheartedly encourage you, if you have other pets in the house, to make sure they are with you when you say goodbye because they need the closure as much as you do. They need to grieve, as Iris explained. Without the closure, they may be wondering where their friend and companion has gone, and that's not fair to them. Their reality is changing as yours is. Including them in the process to help make their transition smoother.

Don't Ask Yourself, "Could I Have Done More?"

This is perhaps one of the hardest pieces of advice to follow:

"Is there anything I could have done to help?"
"Did I miss any signs of a problem?"
"How could I have not seen…?"
"How could I have missed that?"

If you spend time dwelling on these questions, you're not going to solve anything. If anything, you're going to frustrate yourself, second-guessing your actions rather than letting warm memories of your beloved dog wash over your mind, body and heart.

Even if you were to discover something you missed, the outcome will not change; it will not bring your treasured companion back. All it's going to do it make you feel guilty, beating yourself up about "what could have been." If you're really struggling with this piece, set up a reading with Iris or another animal communicator to get some reassurance.

Hindsight is often 20/20, full of clarity and signs that are spotlighted with a flashing red arrow. But for whatever reason, those signs either may not have presented themselves or were not meant to seen.

Spend your mental energy cherishing your memories together rather than worrying about what might have happened. You owe it to your companion, and you owe it to yourself.

Let Yourself Grieve

Having to say goodbye to your dog is a tremendous loss, and there is nothing that is going to immediately fill the void that is left behind. In my experience, if you've been truly connected to your dog, it's almost impossible to turn around and resume a "normal" life right after their death. One of the most important things you can do for yourself is to let yourself grieve.

Give yourself whatever amount of time you need to let your heart heal. What amount of time that is will be different for everyone; there is no magic number of days. This is not the kind of thing you can set a timer on.

How you grieve will be as personal as the amount of time you need. You may decide to journal about some of your favorite memories together, paint or draw a picture of your dog, write a song or a poem, share a tribute on social media or on your blog, create a photo collage for your wall. Surround yourself with things that your dog loved – a favorite toy or their blanket. Share memories, stories, and pictures with others. One of the most beautiful things I experienced when we lost both dogs was the outpouring of love and support from my Facebook community, both friends and strangers. It was an outlet for me to share their beautiful pictures with the world, to share how beautiful they were and what made them so special. In return I was enveloped in love and support from people all around the country and beyond. On the flip side, I can't count how many times I've cried when someone I don't know posted about their own loss; I understand the connection and profound influence they have on our lives, and I felt their loss at some level. So say what you want about social media, but in a situation like this, the support of a broad community of like-minded dog lovers is extremely comforting.

It's Okay To Have Weepy Mornings...

... and afternoons... and evenings.

Here I am now a couple of years out, and I still get teary when I'm left to my thoughts for too long. I can tell you in recent memory the last time I've wept for them – it's right now, as I work on this book. Some days the tears just pool and I manage to blink them away. Other days I give in and mourn their absence. And that's okay.

Unfortunately, especially at first, these occurrences will come on out of the blue, at very unexpected or inopportune times, but to that I advise that you always keep a tissue handy!

Your heart will take time to heal, to whatever extent it can. Let it take the time it needs.

Don't Rush To Erase Their Presence

Being in your house without your beloved dog will feel empty, and there's going to be that strange sensation of being surrounded by their things – their collar and leash, toys, food, bowls, bed and blanket, medicine, chew bones.

Seeing those things will most certainly stir up sadness, but don't rush to put everything away. Turn that sadness into comfort because it is a memory of him or her. Their bedding will smell like them, their bones carry their teeth marks. I still have Bimmer's last chew bone on a shelf next to my desk. Occasionally Minnie will sniff at it, but that's one she can't have. I find comfort it because it was his. Let that component of the healing process take its natural course. Put things away or donate them when it feels right, when your heart is ready.

When you are ready to start packing up the toys and put their bed away, set it aside for that time when you're ready to open your heart to another dog, or consider donating it to a family who would love to share those things with their dog.

Talk To Your Dog

Just because your dog is no longer with your physically, that doesn't mean they are not with you in a different form, as I've shown you throughout this book. So talk to your beloved dog. Tell him or her that you love them and miss them. Say good morning, send them a kiss goodnight. Believe me, they hear you and are excited when you talk to them because they're right with you. And in their own way, they'll respond.

I know that my two are still with me all the time, so why wouldn't I want to talk to them? When you're ready to have the full conversation, reach out to Iris or another animal communicator or Medium.

Be Open To Your Dreams Or Visions

Throughout this book I shared several dreams I've had about Bimmer and Bertram. One I shared earlier was especially comforting to me, the one right I had right after we lost Bertram. I remember very clearly being with her and talking to her. I remember the leaving for the car ride and making sure she got in, had enough room and was comfortable. I remember how the configuration of the car morphed and expanded, as things have a way of doing in dreams – reality and logic don't often play a role. As she settled in next to me on the floor, I clearly remember looking over to my right and one aisle up. My brother's dog, whom he lost, at that point, about five years prior, was facing us, with his head resting on his paws, starting right at me. That's where the dream ended, because that's all I needed to know.

That was my sign that they were together, that he had found Bertram and was with her; she was not alone on the other side.

I got a tremendous sense of peace from that dream.

My sister experienced something similar, but in this case, the sign came from a friend of hers. She had just lost her beloved Poodle, while a friend of hers unexpectedly had to say goodbye to his dog, a brown Chesapeake Bay Retriever. Their dogs were very fond of each other – they got along famously and were each other's favorite play companion. After her loss, her friend called her and told her about a dream he had the night before. He got a call from his credit card company about fraudulent activity on his credit card. He asked who was using his card, and the credit card company representative said it was a Poodle and a brown dog. That was the message that they were together and her dog was being taken care of.

What a comforting thought.

Be open to any signs from your dog. They may come in the form of a dream or a feeling you get when you least expect it. Don't think that because they are not there physically, that you will never hear from them again. Open your mind to the possibility, and you may just receive some sort of message that they are okay and are with other loved ones you have lost – whether it's other pets or people. I know Bimmer and Bertram are together, with my grandmother as their Guardian, and that brings me peace.

Go To Places They Loved

Don't avoid doing things or going places that you used to go with your dog because the memories are too strong or painful. Instead go there and celebrate them, honor their memory.

If you used to go hiking in a particular park, go there and reflect on the times you spent there together. If you used to go to the beach together, go back to the beach and lay a flower in the water. Talk to them while you're there because you know they're right by your side.

No matter where it is, feel them there with you; feel their presence and their energy. Celebrate the time you were there with each other.

Stage 3: Remembrance

There are so many ways that we can remember our sweet companions. They will never leave our hearts, but we can give ourselves a physical reminder of their memory or to serve as a tribute to the impact they made on our lives.

The possibilities are limited only to your imagination. Some are more obvious, while others are inspired by your creativity and your special relationship with your dog.

Photographs

I love smartphones because it's easier than ever to capture exactly the things that make our dogs special to us. We can create digital albums, share pictures on social media, on websites, have the photos printed and framed, create collages, photo canvases, even made into Warhol-like prints. These photos can be put on t-shirts, bags, key chains, and just about anything else you can think of.

Your dog's photo can be your new phone or tablet background photo, and a series of photos can be your computer screensaver.

Donate In Their Honor

One of the most beautiful gifts we received after we lost Bertram came from our vet. They made a donation in her honor to a foundation that provided healthcare to dogs and their owners who could not afford it.

Consider donating to a similar organization, or to your local shelter, rescue group, therapy dog or support dog foundation. Your donation doesn't have to be a large amount, just a little something in their memory because for these organizations, every penny makes a difference.

Capture Everything Special About Your Dog

One common fear when losing a beloved dog is that you'll forget the little things that made them special to you – things that only they did, that made their personality so unique and cherished by you.

Capture each and everything about your dog that made him or her special to you. For me, the way I chose to do this was in writing.

Two days after we lost Bertram I was sitting at my computer trying to work – to no avail. My mind was just not ready, and my thoughts kept going back to her. So I closed what I was working on, opened a clean, blank Word document, and proceeded to list every single thing about Bertram that made her special to me, that made her "my girl." I could not type fast enough, my fingers seemed to dial directly into my brain and took on a mind of their own. Before I knew it, an hour had passed and I had five pages of her magic, captured in words. I added a few things here and there over the next couple of days as I remembered what I missed. I still have that list. I considered adding it in here, but it's far too personal. I don't look at it that often, but when I do, she's right by my side again.

However you choose to capture your dog's unique traits, whether it's in a drawing or painting, in words, in a video, or a voice recording, don't censor your memories. Don't worry if anyone else will like it or understand it. This is for you, and maybe to share with anyone else of your choosing. No one is going to judge or criticize, so let your heart do the talking and take your remembrance where it finds a path.

A Tribute

You may choose to do a tribute to your special dog. Once again, this can take one of many different forms, with no right or wrong way to honor their life and role in your heart. The tribute may come in the form of a celebration or planting a tree in their favorite spot. It may be something more public, like donating balls to a local dog park for others to enjoy.

That's exactly what my friends in California did after they lost their beloved dog. His favorite thing to do was play ball on the beach. After he lost a brave battle with degenerative myelopathy, his people wanted to honor him, so they placed a basket of tennis balls out at his favorite beach, along with a brief story explaining his love for the beach, and encouraging others to take a ball to play with while there. They shared their story on Facebook and with others, and before long, dog owners from around the country were sending tennis balls with their beloved dogs' names on them to place in the basket. While he manned the camera, she would lovingly place the balls in the basket, taking a moment to read the names and locations of each, honoring their place as part of this growing tribute, the videos and photos a special memento for the dog parents.

I knew that one day – I thought far into the future – whenever we did have to say goodbye to one of our goofballs, that I would be sure to honor them by sending balls to include at Forrest's beach. Never did I think that day would come so soon or so suddenly. But early in the morning two days after our losses, we were on our way to buy some tennis balls. We got out some colored Sharpies and carefully decorated each ball with their name, our state, and either a nickname we had for them or a heart or flower. I carefully packed them in a box and sent them off.

We've never been to the beaches of southern California with our two dogs, but I was moved beyond words that Bertram and Bimmer were going to be making some other dogs happy while they played with their special balls on that beach.

I've seen similar memorials at the dog parks here around my house, and each time I stop to read about the dog, and smile because I know they are loving every time someone takes a toy or ball to play with from their basket.

Stage 4: Bringing A New Dog Into Your Heart

Losing your beloved dog leaves a big hole in your heart, but your heart is not forever closed. As hard as it may seem, you will have room in your heart to love another dog. We have such a tremendous capacity to love, and that resource is endless, our hearts just keep expanding. Even though it may seem impossible or too difficult to even think about, one day you will be ready to love another dog.

When Is The Right Time?

There is no set timeframe. A buzzer is not going to go off after 90 days telling you it's time to start looking. You'll know when the time is right. You'll have "that feeling," that sense that you're ready to focus your love and attention on another furry companion. Just like I knew it was the right time to bring Minnie home.

There's no need to rush. If it takes a year, if it takes three. It may only take a few days or a week. That's how long it will take. We're all different, and our relationship with each dog will be different, so it may take a while before you and your future wiggle-butt find each other.

Other people will be free with their opinions and advice of when you should get another dog, usually accompanying by the story of how long before they got another dog, or when their friend or neighbor got a new puppy. That's all good and well for them. Don't let what someone else did sway your heart. If you're not quite prepared, the fit is not going to be right, and that's not fair to you or your furry-legged companion.

You have to be in the right mindset to say, "I'm ready."

The important thing to remember is that, by opening your heart and home to another dog doesn't mean you're "replacing" the beloved companion that you lost. What you're doing is giving your love, heart, affection, attention and companionship to another dog who deserves all those things. Your heart will expand, letting that dog in right beside the other dogs who have been part of your life.

"I Can't Go Through The Pain Of Another Loss."

Loss is a part of life. A very sucky part. We can't live our lives in fear of losing our loved ones – be it people or dogs. We can't deny our love to a dog just because one day, hopefully many years down the road, they will leave us. We don't stop making friends because one day that friend may pass away, do we? Or if we lose a friend or someone we cherish; do we stop forming close connections with other people because you're afraid it will happen again?

No. When you form that special connection with someone – human or canine – you nurture that relationship. You treat it with respect and honor it. You make room in your heart for that relationship.

Loss is an inevitable part of life, but the love and lessons we learn from each relationship is irreplaceable. That is what makes us a better person. A whole person.

With each dog that you bring into your heart, you'll laugh at something new that they do, they will look at you in a way only they can, they will relate to you in a way that is uniquely them. They will teach us new things about ourselves, and help us understand how to relate to each other better. They will teach us about love and patience, about quiet and fun, about anger and forgiveness. Why would you ever want to deny yourself that amazing opportunity? You may even recognize traits or characteristics of your beloved dog in your new dog. Believe it or not, in some cases it may even be your dog, coming back in a new form to be with you again.

Circumstances Change

Maybe at this point in your life you are not able to get another dog just yet. That doesn't mean you can't surround yourself with furry companionship.

You can still get your dog fix by offering to pet sit for friends, or even by fostering a dog for a local rescue group or for organizations. Sign up to be a dog walker on Rover or offer to watch a friend's dog while they go on vacation.

Volunteer at the local shelter or rescue group where you can walk the dogs, help give them care or even play with them. They'll get the love they so deservedly need while they wait for their forever homes.

Heck, if nothing else, go hang out at the local dog park for a couple of hours and play with the dogs there (in a non-stalker kind of way!).

No matter what, there are plenty of ways to get your fix of furry companionship.

And when your circumstances change and you're ready, your new fuzz-ball will find you.

Why does watching a dog be a dog
fill one with happiness?
~ Jonathan Safran Foer

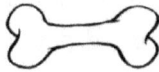

Our Souls Will Meet Again

Once you have a wonderful dog,
A life without one, is a life diminished.
~ Dean Koontz

The story doesn't end here, to that I'm positive. My Spiritual journey is only beginning, and I continue to have visits from my beloved Bimmer and Bertram, and my grandmother is guiding me as I travel my new path (and making sure I don't stray too far off course). They continue to play a big role in Minnie's life, mentoring her and teaching her about life and love.

Although they still flow, I have long since stopped apologizing for my tears, even the sudden, uncontrollable eruptions of grief that pop up in the weirdest places at random times: in line at the grocery store, while driving – all the time, in the middle of a charity dinner event, while scrolling through posts on Facebook when my mind is too quiet, while reading or making dinner. They still happen. I experienced a loss that ran so deep and so wide, and I am not ashamed of how those beautiful souls impacted my life. So, I let the tears come, and just move on when they eventually dry up (although I have to say, that's one of the reasons I now have tattooed eyeliner!).

This is not the story I originally started to write. *Dogs Still Know Best* was going to be very different, a "truer" sequel, where more lessons from Bimmer and Bertram (and some special guests) were shared. But as our lives changed and we had to adapt to our new reality, so did the story. It no longer made sense to tell it that way. I now know I was meant to tell a very different one that more accurately reflects my journey. Hopefully along the way I'm able to help others who experience deep loss in their lives.

They say soul groups travel together across lifetimes. It gives me an enormous amount of comfort knowing that, somehow, somewhere, in some form, I will again be reunited with my sweet angels. Until then, I'll cherish every sign, every feather, every scent and sense that they are with me, guiding both me and Minnie as we navigate together the physical world they left behind. I see their influence on Minnie and it makes me smile. They are still together, "really enjoying being here and keeping an eye on you and doing the doggie things there are to do on this side," according to Bimmer. With Iris' help and a lot of self-study and effort, I am continuing to do everything I can to improve and enhance my own abilities to communicate with them.

It is part of my life's path to wholeheartedly embrace this journey and travel it with as much kindness, gentleness, openness and love as possible. I will continue to learn, meditate, practice and enhance my abilities as much as I can. I will seek the help of those who can guide me to a deeper connection, and I will continue to share my experiences on the chance that I can help even one other person to heal their heart, get in touch with their abilities or even acknowledge their experiences.

I am excited for the messages, lessons and visits I'll be receiving in the future, because I know they'll come. They will come not only from my two angels, but from my grandmother, my guides and entire team of Spirit cheerleaders. I also know I'll be having a lot more conversations with Minnie, learning more about how her complex mind works, how she experiences her life around her and how we can continue to be as strong together as a team as possible.

Open your mind, open your heart, open your eyes. Look for the messages and signs that your loved ones are sending to you each day because they're there. If you can block out the noise of life for even a moment and quiet your heart, you'll surely be rewarded with a gift that will make you smile. Who knows, you may even start a journey of your own.

"Your wings were ready,
but my heart was not."
~ Unknown

Interview Transcript: Iris, Angie and Minnie

What follows is a transcript of Minnie's reading with Iris Matos in July, 2018 at my house. I wanted you to have a chance to experience the whole conversation from all sides. I am so grateful that I chose to record the session so I will forever have her words, which I think you'll find, are ones to treasure. I hugged Minnie hard that evening and thanked her. I didn't sleep much that night; I kept waking up and thinking about her words with a smile on my face.

My advice to you? If you ever have the opportunity to have a reading done with your beloved dog (or cat, dog, turtle, ferret, bird, frog, fish…) with Iris or another trusted animal communicator, make sure you record it and then have it transcribed so you forever have a very special memento.

August 2018

Iris: So, even though I'm here, she [Minnie] is going to go off and do things and I'll still be communicating with her because they can multitask, so it's not like she has to be paying attention to me or even to you to communicate.

Angie: Okay.

Iris: So, you will hear some silences, we have been through this process before, while I am talking to her and waiting for her to respond. I am asking her to show me something that you would understand, that you would know that it would definitely be her. Is there a little white dog, with a lot of energy, kind of a yippy, loud…

Angie: Our neighbor! Right next door, a little Westie.

Iris: Yep! Okay, fluffy, kinda has the little beard thing going. I asked her to show me somebody that she likes, so they are buddies… except she says he is really loud sometimes. Well thank you, thank you very much for showing me that. I'll do a little bit more of that since she is already here, so what questions do you have for Minnie?

Angie: Is she happy?

Iris: The immediate answer was yes, so I asked her to show me a little bit more about what her experience is here. She feels comfortable; she feels loved, she knows that she is safe with you, she is secure, "and they love me no matter what I do."

Angie: That's true.

Iris: So, she feels really free to be herself and to do different things. I've got goosebumps from head to toe right now so that's my validation, that's how I know that I am on the right track. She feels free to take risks, try different things and in fact, you guys encourage her to do so and she really likes that, she enjoys that freedom. I'm asking her if there is anything else she wants to show me about being here. She gets to meet really interesting people, okay so I think this is her, every day is a new adventure; there are adventures in this house and the reason I say I think this is her is because my mom used to say "we're going on an adventure!"

Angie: Yes, we do.

Iris: Okay, so I just want to make sure, okay, so I ask… when I come across something like that I'll ask myself… I'll ask, "Is this me or is this the animal that I am talking to?" and then I'll just get an answer, so it's the animal, but I wanted to double check. It's always an adventure; she likes going on adventures.

Angie: Because that is one thing, I know she is smart and she gets bored and I want her to go different places, and we do things together. I do I always think of different things we can do or different places we can go.

Iris: And she appreciates that. Such a bond… I'm seeing her, she is running and her ears kinda flow back like a cape, is what she is showing me, and she's again it's that freedom she really enjoys. That freedom of the running and going to different places. You guys don't always go to the same place/park. There is one that's close, and she is showing me the car ride in terms of her sense of time, so there is one that you can get to very quickly that she really likes, but there is one that you drive a ways to, she has to lay down to get to, and that's her favorite...

Angie: That's her favorite?

Iris: The one that you have to drive to, she says "I have to lay down..."

Angie: The one where she has to lay down, that could be either Twinsburg or that could be where we go barn hunt, because that is in Kirtland so that's almost an hour drive.

Iris: So yeah, because it feels long.

Angie: That's probably Kirtland, and that would be her favorite because that's where she barn hunts and gets to find the rats.

Iris: Okay.

Angie: [Speaking to Minnie] Is that what you mean then? Do you mean where you go find the ratties and go see Janice?

Iris: Um, when you said Janice, I felt a little spike of energy in her.

Angie: [To Minnie] Oh, you do like her, don't you? We will have to tell her that!

Iris: Yes, yes, she does.

Angie: [To Minnie] She's a nice lady, huh?

Iris: So, the answer is yes, she really loves it here; she is really happy, she feels free to be herself and free to take chances, that's basically the summary of that question. She likes to go on the adventures and just loves the barn hunting, it's fun for her.

Angie: Now, does she say why she gets scared going into daycare?

Iris: I'll ask her about it. What I am going to ask her is what her experience is with that. [Pause] Those voices, and that's what she is calling them, not barks but voices, they reverberate in her body so like it goes into... she is a very open, very sensitive, she picks things up, energies, and very she's empathic from what I can feel, so those voices really get into her and so that's she says. "When I was young I was not aware of it" because it was more in her head.

Angie: She's coming into her own now. I can feel that she has a real sensitive soul; I can feel that with her.

Iris: So, as she's opening up and opening herself up to the world, it has become *more*... Hmm... so we gotta' figure out how we can work around that.

Angie: That's good to know though!

Minnie: [Barking]

Iris: You go girl, go get 'em. I can try and talk to her about protection?

197

Angie: That would be good; that would be great!

Iris: She's not understanding the protection thing, because I'm telling her that... what I said to her was... there is a way that you can sort of close that off so it does not hurt you so much and then open it up again when you are finished, but she does not get that, she's not understanding and she is just thinking okay so you are open, open, open, you're open, that's it.

Angie: And maybe with her age and maturity she might begin to understand that?

Iris: Understand that, as we get older, we do understand that it's not all black and white.

Angie: Okay, that's good.

Iris: So, she is still black and white. How old is she again?

Angie: She'll be 20 months on August 4th.

Iris: Okay, so she really is still just a pup.

Angie: She's just a pup, yes, she is very puppy-like.

Angie: Okay, [Whistle] Minnie, come! Come here! Good girl, what else should we talk about? Does she feel good?

Iris: She feels her body is strong, she feels strong... she feels invincible like there is absolutely nothing she can't do.

Angie: [Laughing] Why doesn't that surprise me?

Iris: And at some point, she is going to find her limitations. She's like, "Now I can do whatever I want, whenever I want. I'm strong!" I'm asking her to show me, in my body, if there are any pains or any issues she has come across. I feel like she has had a tummy upset recently.

Angie: Yeah, she has.

Iris: But that seems to have worked itself out; that it's not bothering her anymore. She said, "That was not fun! Not fun at all because I didn't know what was going on and I didn't like it."

Angie: She woke up yesterday with a really, really loud tummy. it was just loud, she didn't have diarrhea, she wasn't sick, but it was loud. I felt so bad.

Iris: I feel like it was gas that couldn't come out.

Angie: Okay, yeah, that would be uncomfortable.

Iris: Yeah and she was not pleased, not at all happy with that and I would not be either.

Angie: No. Is there any wisdom or lessons she wants to share with me?

Iris: She feels like she is here to help you have fun, because you seem to have forgotten that for a little while, just how to have fun. So, while you are getting her out, she's getting you out. And there is joy in life that is always there, and you just have to see it. You don't have to look for it, you don't have to find it, you just have to see it, and she is here to help you see it – the joy and beauty in life that is right in front of you.

Angie: That's beautiful! Does she talk with Bimmer and Bertram?

Iris: All the time, all the time she goes "I'm in training, I'm in training."

Angie: [Laughing]

Iris: Which one [Bimmer or Bertram] was the strong one?

Angie: Bertram.

Iris: Okay, she is… okay, sometimes they use images, and that we know they look inside us and find images, and she is showing me the Jedi master with the Padawan, and that's Bertram and her, so she is really feeling like that wisdom that Bertram had and shared with you.

Angie: [To Minnie] She's your mentor, huh?

Iris: She really is. Though she said they don't come around as much as they did when she was little, and I mean little like a wee one. So, she doesn't know if she is close to graduating yet; she doesn't feel grown up in herself yet, so she's hoping that they keep coming around.

Angie: They will, they'll keep coming. The dove has been around a lot, the Mourning Dove, and that's one of their signs for me. She's been around a lot and she will just sit on the end of the railing and look at me.

Iris: Yeah, so I'm asking if there is anything else she wants to share about that particular experience. She says "No, we can't share all of our secrets yet."

Angie: Ha ha, stinker! That's fair. Can I make a request of her maybe? When we barn hunt, her indication to tell me she found the tube with a rat in it used to be so strong, but now it's gotten really subtle. Fortunately, I can read her indication, but it's gotten really subtle and we're starting now to do competitions. So, if you can remind her that when she finds a rat, we have to work as a team, she can't just find it herself and then mosey on.

Iris: Okay, this is me asking. What is the indication that you want her to use? So I can show it to her, I can show her an image.

Angie: She can either bark or dig.

Iris: And what one would you prefer, or either?

Angie: Yeah, whatever she is most comfortable with. [To Minnie] We work as a team because you do all the hard work, but I speak English and I have to tell the judge what you're telling me.

Iris: So, what I'm showing her is finding what she is looking for, and when she finds what she's looking for, she has to give a very strong bark or she needs to dig deep, so I'm showing her what that looks like. And what I'm saying is, if she wants to continue to compete and do well, this is what she needs to let you know, so I'm giving her a reason as well.

Angie: Okay, good.

Iris: I kid you not, this is exactly what she just did, kinda like Genie doing her little head nod, she said okay, and apparently, she got it. This Thursday you will have to let me know how she does.

Angie: I will.

Iris: Because I kid you not that's exactly what she did, very emphatic. She thinks this is cool, she likes this.

Angie: What we're doing now?

Iris: Mhm, yep, she's like, "So I tell you stuff and you say it in those words?" And I'm like, "Yes."

Angie: Okay! Oh no!

Iris: She's like, "Can anybody do this?" I'm like, "Yeah, if they work at it, if they train at it and they are open to this." "Can mama do this?"

Angie: [gasp]

Iris: So, um, I'll give you a few tips so once I leave here… so that you can hear her.

Angie: [To Minnie] Mama really wants to do this with you, sweetheart.

Iris: She refers to Tom as Dad.

Angie: Good.

Iris: She thinks he is hilarious, so I'm going to ask you a question: is he a little less disciplinary than you are? Because they have fun, so much fun. And there is so much love there between them. There is fun and there's love. He is strong, very strong personality-wise very strong physically, so they can play a little bit rougher.

Angie: And they do.

Iris: And that makes her feel good, because she feels like she is helping him stay strong.

Angie: Oh, yeah, she's doing good work because I'm the one that's always going, "Gentle, easy, gentle!" doing the Mom-thing.

Iris: So, you're a family, this is a family, not just a pack, but a family.

Angie: Does she like the fact that I talk to her all day?

Iris: Yes. She said it exactly like that. "It would be boring if you didn't talk to me all day, I would wonder what is wrong with you." She's got a little bit of an attitude, this one.

Angie: Yes, she does! She's a sassy one. She's smart and she knows it. My other two were smart, but she is *very* smart. I mean, you see it in her eyes. You can just see her thinking, thinking, thinking, it's like Pooh Bear when he goes, "Think, think, think, think." That's what I think she is doing because she is constantly looking and sniffing and investigating and learning her world and learning how to gain the system, is my impression, [laugh] to her advantage.

Iris: I don't know, she was with you until you said "gain the system." She was all in on that one and then when you said "gain the system," she said, "I don't know if that's true." She does not know if that's true, she is just trying to figure out the world.

Angie: Figure out the world. Okay, that's fair. So, I took it too far?

Iris: Yeah. I'm trying to understand something. Hold on, give me a second... [Pause] She says she will press her advantage if she knows that is what's best.

Angie: Yeah, so I wasn't far off.

Iris: It's not, but it's not a selfish thing, though. She will press the advantage if she has the advantage; she will press it if it's the right thing for her, for you, for Tom. It's not just solely selfishness.

Angie: She doesn't strike me as selfish.

Iris: Yeah, so you didn't get it completely wrong; she will do that, but she will not internalize it. She will do it if it is what's best, period. So if she feels you're not getting enough time outside or if you're not finding that joy and that's her job to help you find that joy, she will use every tool at her disposal.

Angie: And she does; she is persistent. Does she understand why I'm trying to crate train her.

Iris: That's a big fat no, Nope! Doesn't get it! So, we can talk about that.

Angie: Okay, I don't need it for home, but when we go to scent work class and, it's not her turn she has to wait quietly in a crate, and I sit next to her. Same thing when she gets more into competitions and she may have to wait before it's her turn and we don't want to wait in the car, if we have a crate, I would be right next to her.

Iris: Okay, she goes, "It's for doing the work?" That was her question.

Angie: Yes.

Iris: Okay I'm showing her sitting quietly in her crate and I'm showing her you are sitting next to her and luckily, I have been to competitions, so I know what the setup looks like.

Angie: I would be in a chair right next to her.

Iris: She says she will try harder.

Angie: Good. The first time we got to class I didn't know we would have to do that so we sort of fumbled through it and it was unexpected for both of us. We worked really hard on it during the week and when we went to class last week, everyone complimented how well she done because she did about 30 minutes with pretty good patience, and then her anxiety built up and the more it built, the more anxious she got. But I've had three women compliment her on how good she did, so I'm hoping she understands that is when we have to wait our turn and we can go work and so she's safe and the other dogs are safe.

Iris: She said, "Okay, I'll work harder on that."

Angie: [To Minnie] **"Good girl!"** [Angie sprayed a cooling solution on a spot between her toes] She's got a little itchy spot between her toes and I think from allergies, and I just got this from Wondercide, it's an itch and allergy skin tonic; it's all natural for pets and people. I put it on her when we got home from daycare and it seemed to do really well, she left it alone.

Iris: Oh! We could try that with my puppy, Athens has allergies.

Angie: And it smells good!

Iris: That makes a difference!

Angie: So hopefully that helps her because I know it kept her up overnight, and I know it's one of those things where there's an itch between her toes and she licks it and it itches more and she licks it and it cycles.

Iris: Yep!

Angie: [To Minnie] "Well, thank you sweetie, we'll do well in your crate; I know it's a weird thing but I'll be right there with you." [To Iris] I knew she would be a chatty one!

Iris: I'm still connected with her. When you sprayed the stuff on her toes it felt cooling.

Angie: Oh, that's good, I was hoping it would be cooling.

Iris: it felt cooling, um almost like minty.

Angie: Good, that's good.

Iris: I don't know If I explained that properly?

Angie: No, I get that reference completely!

Iris: Good! I don't have to understand anything.

Angie: Makes perfect sense, minty can be cooling. "Finally found something that makes you feel better, huh?" Bimmer had very sensitive skin, I've heard that from other Pointer owners and even with white Boxers and such…

Iris: [To Minnie] You have fabulous ears.

Angie: … the predominantly white dogs tend to be more sensitive and even emotionally sensitive. That explains her being very empathic yet having some allergy problems.

Iris: Yes, having some allergy problems. [Minnie put her head in Iris' lap] She thinks she is beautiful because she is beautiful. She said, "I am so pretty."

Angie: [Laughing] And I tell her that all the time! I tell her she is a supermodel, she Is the supermodel of the dog world because other Pointers are pretty, but Min is exceptional. And I tell her that, she is beautiful inside and out, she has got a beautiful soul and a beautiful spirit.

Iris: She wholeheartedly agrees.

Angie: Humble is not the word to use for Minnie.

Iris: Maybe that will come with age, who knows?

Angie: Um, it kinda doesn't.

Iris: [To Minnie] Okay, are we friends now? Now that I rubbed your ears?

Angie: "I told you good things about her; you say thank you?"

Iris: Okay, I got a nose bump and the tail wiggle.

Angie: That's exceptional, to get the tail wiggle. That's a good sign.

Iris: I'm asking her if there is anything else she wants to tell you, and she says, "We understand each other pretty well."

Angie: I think we do. We do, huh?

Iris: She said that she is excited that I am going to try and teach you some tips and so you can hear her; she said, "That's cool, I would like that."

Angie: [To Minnie] We make a good team, don't we, Min?

Iris: She said the exact same thing.

Angie: Aww. We *do* make a good team, right? Thank you, sweetheart, thank you for sharing everything.

Iris: She wants to know if there are any more questions you have.

Angie: The big ones were daycare, making sure you felt good, were happy, were healthy, what wisdom she had for me. I'm glad she likes the parks and to play, the indication at barn hunt was when I wanted to get help with that so we can understand each other.

Iris: She wants to do a good job; she really wants to do a good job, she wants to do well.

Angie: She does. When there are things that she does that I tell her, like if she stands up on the counter and I say, "Minnie, no, down!" or if she takes a shoe and I tell her, "No," and she does it just over and over and over, is she just playing with me or am I not telling her the right words?

Iris: She knows what she is supposed to do, she just kinda forgets, so just reiterating it is working because it's getting in there, it's just a matter of, she gets excited and she forgets then she is reminded and she's like, "Oh! Yeah, Okay." And then, bright shiny, and it's like, "Oh look, there it is again!"

Angie: Okay! I do have a question and this one puzzles me so if she could help me understand, because we let her out and you know it's a busy road so we let her go out on the deck to go potty, and she's been great with that since she was a puppy, and she's got her door. But when it rains and the deck is wet, not even raining just when the deck is wet, I have to take her to the front yard to tinkle, why is that?

Iris: It feels slimy.

Angie: Okay! But why will she go in the grass? Because the grass is wet.

Iris: It's a texture thing, so like that feels safe when its dry, it feels solid. But when it's wet it feels a little slimy or slippery; "No just no," that's what she just said [laughing].

Angie: [Laughing] Okay! I've learned to just accept it.

Iris: She said, "I can't handle it, I don't like it, I don't feel safe."

Angie: Like this morning, it rained overnight, it was not raining when we woke up, it was 5:30. I just put on her collar and leash and took her out the front, I didn't even bother to ask.

Iris: No, because it just feels slippery, so she does not feel secure, so squatting down to pee. She was very emphatic about the "Just no!" [laughing]

Angie: Okay! And I know because it's one of those things she'll go out there with me, and she'll stand there and look at me like, "Are you ready? Are you ready to go inside?" [To Minnie] "I know your toe itches, you'll get your allergy medicine for overnight."

Iris: She says, "Thank you, thank you very much." Do you have any other questions?

Angie: I don't, those were the big ones, as long as she is happy, healthy, nothing pressing she needs to tell me. If you could help her to maybe not lick her toe so to help it heal?

Iris: I try that with mine, it does not work. I can tell her what's going to happen.

Angie: Okay! [laughing] I told her she will have to wear a sock or a cone. [To Minnie] "So, are we good now, Min?"

Iris: She's good. [To Minnie] "So thank you, sweetie, thank you for talking to me." I always say thank you and I ask if it's okay if I come back?

Angie: I hope she said yes?

Iris: Yes, she did. I have never had anybody say no to me.

Angie: [laughing] I can't imagine they would!

Iris: She just asked if she's going to have babies?

Angie: [To Minnie] Oh, no sweetheart, you're not going to have babies. But someday you'll most likely have a brother or sister that you can play with, would you like that?

Iris: She said, "Okay, yes I would, but I'm not ready yet. I'm still learning."

Angie: Oh! I do have one last question… I have a low file drawer on the side of my desk, and I keep my crystals and stones. Minnie is so drawn to them, she can't leave them alone some days.

Iris: She said they are a beacon to her. She is completely drawn to them, they are a beacon.

Angie: That's what I figured because it's not like she's sniffing at the boxes or things around them… it's definitely the stones themselves. And there are definitely ones that she is more drawn to than others.

Iris: Do you have any other questions?

Angie: No, I think that's a lot. Thank you, sweet girl, for talking with us!

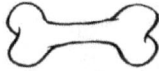

Interview Transcript: Iris, Angie and Minnie

Angie: Alright, this is Iris and Minnie part 3, are you ready, Girlie? I already told you what we are going to do.

Iris: You see her brain just goes and goes and goes and goes, so she has got loads of things going on in that noggin' of hers. So, no wonder you cannot sit still, Sweetheart.

Angie: You can tell there is a lot going on in her head.

Iris: Yeah. It's constant, it's hard for her to settle sometimes. Like even when she is asleep her brain is going so she is trying to figure out a lot of things. Just with her surroundings and her environment there is something new in the air all the time for her. She can smell how things change, and that is why she is so fascinated with my bag because there are a lot of scents on that.

Angie: Ohh, sure.

Iris: So, it's not just my dogs, it's my workplace, my car and all these different things.

Angie: Right.

Iris: So, I am in contact with a lot of animals so I'm sure their scents are on there.

Angie: [To Minnie] You have a lot going on in that brain of yours, huh?

Iris: You do have a big brain. So, she just wanted to let you know that if it looks like she is not paying attention or it seems like she is somewhere else, she is processing information. Which is fascinating but not surprising knowing her, knowing how complex she is. She is not a simple puppy.

Angie: No, not by any means.

Iris: [Minnie runs to the door] Although that's pretty solidly, "I need to go out." [Both laughing] Do you need me to pause this?

Angie: We can pause, yeah. [To Minnie a few minutes later] Feel better?

Iris: So much! I tried to stay connected with her while she was out there because I don't want to you know have her going back and forth, but she disconnected with me, she was like, "I'll be right back, give me a sec."

Angie: Does she have any idea what caused the allergic outbreak she had a couple of weeks ago?

Iris: No clue. She has no idea what it was, she thinks it was something she ate but she is not fully sure. It was hot, everything was hot, is what she keeps telling me. It was itchy and it was hot, she was just hot.

Angie: She was hot, that's why I think she had a fever.

Iris: Poor thing. She is saying it was like she couldn't get away from the heat and it was just frustrating.

Angie: Is she feeling better now?

Iris: Oh yeah. She is fine. I am doing a quick body scan here.

Angie: Mhm.

Iris: She still has little flare ups, but it hasn't been that bad again. Every now and then something just flares up and then it cools down again. So, I am asking her "has she eaten something when she gets those flare ups?" and she says she has been trying to keep track and she just can't figure it out. Which is kind of interesting that she is that fore thoughted about it.

Angie: [To Minnie, who is barking] Come here sweetie, you're fine.

Angie: Now we haven't been to barn hunt in the last two weeks. We're going Thursday, but we didn't go the last two weeks because I know she was eating the straw and it was making her sick. So, we stopped going for a couple of weeks and we are going to try Thursday, but if she continues to eat the straw we are not going to be able to barn hunt anymore. I won't take her to barn hunt because I don't want her to get sick.

Iris: Okay.

Angie: I think she eats it out of frustration is what I think.

Iris: Mhm, I am asking her what her experience is with barn hunt and the straw. I am getting a picture of like a square and there is like a railing somewhere. So, what I am seeing is like a white square.

Angie: Yes, that's the ring.

Iris: And then there is like a railing. When she is looking at where the ring is and it's kind of all lit up, is that where the straw is?

Angie: Yeah.

Iris: Okay because it's all lit up so it's really attractive to her. So, I am asking her why she feels the need to eat it. She said because if it's that bright out there, it's going to be even brighter inside of her. And I am explaining to her no, this is what is making you ill and this is why you have not been going to work. She thought that if she ate enough of it then it would be okay. And I am explaining to her that no, that's not how it works, if it made her sick once then it will continue to make her sick. (Sorry I got a little bit distracted by your cupboard under the stairs there, I was going to ask you if Harry Potter was in there.)

Angie: [Laughing] That door goes to our basement.

Iris: She is laughing at me. She said "You get distracted by bright shiny things too!" Yes, yes I do.

Angie: Haha, you two are quite a pair. Alright, both of you focus.

Iris: [Laughing] did you see that look I got? Alright back to it.

Angie: Back to straw and barn hunt.

Iris: We were at the straw and it's not good for you. If it's going to make you sick once it's going to continue to make you sick.

Angie: [To Minnie] And if you get sick, we can't keep going because I cannot have you sick, Honey. I don't want to do that to you, but I know you have fun.

Iris: She misses working, she does. She feels lazy.

Angie: [To Minnie] You feel lazy? So, we are going to go this week, we are going to go in two days back to work, but you have to try and not eat the straw. Could you try that?

Iris: Big sigh, okay.

Angie: But then we will go back to work because in two weeks you have a competition and if you eat the straw, you can't go the competition.

Iris: She wanted to know if the competition is where everybody is there? Like the whole entire world is there, because that is how she puts it.

Angie: Yeah, there will be a lot of people there. Dad will probably be there.

Iris: Oh!

Angie: Yeah, she likes when Dad watches.

Iris: Yeah, she said, "Dad is very proud of me"

Angie: Yes, he is.

Iris: She said "I love Dad!"

Angie: Aww, he loves you too.

Iris: "Where is Dad?"

Angie: He's upstairs!

Iris: "He is too quiet."

Angie: He is probably sleeping. His back hurts, he hurt his back. Go upstairs Min, you can go see him and you can go snuggle with him. Yeah. He's got that blanket you like.

Iris: You can, we can still talk when you are upstairs if you want. She is like, "no I am good." Okay, she said she will try to not eat the straw.

Angie: Good.

Iris: "But it's so bright though!"

Angie: It won't be brighter in your tummy. (Alright you can have a couple more of these treats, we will give them to Iris while you talk and we will save the rest for when she leaves.)

Iris: Good girl, look how nice you are.

Angie: Now along with the barking, she knows you and she knew you were coming but she let out a big bark and she scares people because she has a big bark and she goes right up to them.

Iris: Have you spoken to her about being a lady, is that something that resonates with you?

Angie: Being a lady? We haven't talked specifically about being a lady.

Iris: So, is this something you have learned from the other two? She says "I have to learn to be a lady, it's hard." So I am showing her the expected behavior when somebody comes in, sit quietly next to you but it is really hard for her, there is all this energy that wants to come out. So I am now asking her what you could do to help her to learn how the be a lady. She does not have any ideas on that.

Angie: Would it help her if I told her when people are okay and people are safe and then if I need her to go into protection mode, I could tell her to go to protection, otherwise when we meet somebody new or see somebody even if its unexpected... and we have talked about this before, she does not like surprises in her environment.

Iris: No, she doesn't.

Angie: I won't let people touch her because I know she does not want to be touched or petted because people are attracted to her and want to come up and say hi but when she barks, they interpret it as aggressive. If they are not real dog people and they get scared.

Iris: She says "I'm not scary!" Yeah, you are!

Angie: She is. [Laughing]

Iris: So what I am doing is showing her what it is like for me when I come in the door and she is acting that way so it kind of scares me, and it's hard for me to come in and say hello to you… and I was really excited to say hello to you but I couldn't act the way I wanted to because she was barking and jumping up. She says, "Oh, I never thought about the way that it affects Mom or other people.

Angie: (I have to retrieve a slipper that she took, I'm still listening.)

Iris: Okay. I'm trying to get her to acknowledge that she needs to change her behavior, but she hasn't quite gotten there yet, but she understands now, she understands how it feels for other people. So, she does have empathy if she understands how it feels for other people.

Angie: Well how about if I put it this way to her, when

we go somewhere, and she is next to me people see her and they see a beautiful dog. So, they like to come up to me and talk to me about her and what I am trying to do is make sure they don't pet her but they still want to talk... what's her name, how old is she, tell me about her... and if she acts out like that then I have to walk away and they don't even get a chance to see how pretty she is.

Iris: So I am explaining that to her, I'm showing her what the expected behavior is and that nobody is actually going to touch her. But this is the way that you socialize and this is the way you get to meet people.

Angie: Yeah that is one of the things she liked, she liked that I get to meet people through her.

Iris: Yeah so, the other thing I am going to explain to her is that you don't need her to protect you and you guys are partners and if you need her, you will let her know.

Angie: And then I want her to go into full protection mode.

Iris: Right but it is going to be more of a matter of when you tell her. So did we talk about a safe word yet?

Angie: No.

Iris: Okay, so you guys can work out what it is. So when everything is okay, you use that word or whatever that word is.

Angie: Min, what word do you want to use as a safe word?

Iris: She is telling me "It's good"

Angie: I was going to say "It's okay." So we will use "It's good."

Iris: Great, it will take some practice.

Angie: That's okay, right, we can practice Min? There are two women in one of our classes that she doesn't like much. I don't know if they just catch her off guard, like they stand up or she sees them move around too much, because if everybody is in their place when we walk in then she is fine, but not for these two particular women, so we can practice with them in nose work class. So, we will practice with them on Friday?

Iris: Yep, she is good with that.

Angie: Okay, and I will tell you if everything is okay, I will say "it's good." But you like scent work class?

Iris: She loves all the classes, she loves them all, it gives her a purpose so she does not feel so lazy. [Both laughing] She said, "I have a tendency to wallow in my laziness."

Angie: [Laughing] How do you figure you are lazy?

Iris: She is not moving every second of every day.

Angie: But that's okay, Min!

Iris: "No! You got to go, you got to do, you got to go, you got to do." That's what she keeps saying.

Angie: So, you were very happy that we went to play ball this afternoon.

Iris: Mhm, she is showing me her running with the ball and when her ears go back she thinks that's fun and funny, almost like they are pinned.

Angie: Yeah! What kind of dogs does she like and not like? Because I am trying to pick up patterns and she clearly likes little dogs and I think she tends to like females.

Iris: Yeah when you said what dogs does she like immediately I saw little ones, little white fluffy ones.

Angie: What kind of dogs don't you like?

Iris: Any kind of dog that is bigger than her.

Angie: Boys and girls?

Iris: Yeah, especially if they are dark, like she cannot clearly make out their eyes or features.

Angie: Okay! That is interesting to know.

Iris: Yeah, she can't quite get them, she can't quite define them or make them out. So, like if they are fluffy and black, that's even worse. Fluffy, black and bigger than her, get out!

Angie: Newfys… Bad combination!

Iris: Yeah [laughing] so if they are bigger than her or darker than her. Fluffys are okay along as they are smaller than her. Because then she can stand over them and figure out what they are. So I think Siena would probably be okay if she wasn't such a jerk, but I think she would be okay because she is small.

Angie: Right.

Iris: So even if she is dark, it's okay.

Angie: Yeah but her face also has definition. So it's going to be interesting when we go to (canine) camp with Skye and Tricia because Skye is bigger, fluffy and dark and a boy! So what Trish and I actually talked about was maybe having you help us so we can all talk together before we go to camp.

Iris: Yeah that's probably a good idea.

Angie: And then what we will have is she will probably come up like a couple days ahead and meet in a neutral place - not here because this is Minnie's territory – meet somewhere neutral because Skye is also like the boy, he is kind of a goofball and plays hard, and she does not tend to like that. She doesn't like when other dogs play rough with, her but he is a big fluffy dark male so we will probably need some intervention from a paid professional.

Iris: [Laughing] We will have to work that one out, It didn't even occur to me about that so, yeah.

Angie: That's actually been on my brain for a while because June is going to creep up and we are planning on driving up together because Skye rides in the car in his crate, but that is still a lot of together time. And once we are there I am not as worried, but I would still like them to get along, but on paper we are going to have an issue.

Iris: Yeah, we will have to explain to her that it is her cousin and it will happen more often in her lifetime so we will have that discussion when It gets a little bit closer.

Angie: Now is there a way they can be like introduced to each other, if she sees pictures or whatever?

Iris: That I actually don't know, I will have to research that.

Angie: And we can experiment too.

Iris: The look on her face is definitely, "What the bark?"

Angie: So, ask her what's up with her nails? Why we can't file her nails down?

Iris: It feels like little electric shocks because of the allergies, so like that's where her flare ups, it happens in her paws, so that when you are trying to file them it's like little shocks.

Angie: Even when (the groomer) does it?

Iris: Yeah, that's what it feels like.

Angie: So her allergy flareups are in her paws.

Iris: Yes.

Angie: That explains why she was licking her paws... so it's not actually the sensation of the file but more so the allergies?

Iris: Yeah. The allergy. So once you get that sorted. [Did she just open the door to come inside on her own?!]

Angie: Yes.

Iris: That's amazing! I'm glad my dogs can't do that.

Angie: I think she does it for fun like if I am working she will come and make me go play with her. Min, tell her about your door closing. She'll go in a room and close the door, locking herself in.

Iris: Alright... well, I have never heard her say this kind of language before...

Angie: Oh no...

Iris: She says, "It freaks mom the fuck out!"

Angie: [Laughing] Did she just say that?!

Iris: She did [Laughing].

Angie: Minifred!

Iris: She totally did, and she was laughing! She's what, 2 years old now?

Angie: Yeah, she is just about 2 now.

Iris: So she is a teenager.

Angie: And I know she is doing it just purely for entertainment.

Iris: Yep!

Angie: She did it five times yesterday, she kept going in the bathroom and she closed the door all the way.

Iris: She said, "It's a ghost!"

Angie: [Laughing] Oh my gosh, okay, that was hilarious, but she is happy otherwise she feels good?

Iris: Yeah, she just misses going to work.

Angie: We are going to work in another couple of days, so we have another competition coming up for nose work and then we have barn hunt work, so you are going to be doing a lot of work.

Iris: She said she enjoys the nose work more than the barn hunt.

Angie: Really?! Do you? You like the nose work better?

Iris: She said it's more challenging. Is that true?

Angie: Yes.

Iris: It's more difficult, it uses up more of her brain capacity. She is trying to explain it... so it takes more thinking to get through what she needs to do and she enjoys that challenge. She likes learning things.

Angie: That has a lot more new things to learn than barn hunt because the only thing that changes with barn hunt is a different number of rats and the tunnel changes, those are the only variables but with nose work there can be four different scents it can be in containers, in a box... in rows of boxes and she has to pick out the right one, it can be in a room somewhere, it can be in a vehicle, it can be outside or inside, interiors so there is a lot of variables.

Iris: Yeah, she enjoys that very much. She is a thinker.

Angie: [To Minnie] What else do you want me to know, Honey?

Iris: "I like talking to you."

Angie: I like talking to you too, Min!

Iris: She said that she gets you and you get her and let her be who she is, and I am pretty sure she said that before. I don't know, but it sounds familiar.

Iris: There is music, she has got music in her head. Almost like a waltz... its instrumental and it feels like a waltz, that kind of timing. I don't know where its coming from though.

Angie: Does she like that music?

Iris: Yes.

Angie: Yeah? We can put more music on when we drive. We can play classical music in the car.

Iris: Yeah, just not rock, she likes classical. She said, Thanks, momma."

Angie: Well that I can do, that's easy to do.

Iris: That's a new one.

Angie: Yeah, she is, she is very complex for a 2-year-old.

Iris: Yes [laughing]! So I am asking her if there is anything else she wants you to know, and she is saying no. She will try to keep up her parts of the bargain.

Angie: I will remind you, and I am going to keep trying to get better at talking to you, I am, I'm trying.

Iris: [Minnie doing something cute] That's adorable.

Angie: I know.

Iris: That really is utterly adorable.

Angie: Do you wonder why I have 8,000 pictures of her?

Iris: I know, I have the same problem, I literally could not stop taking pictures of my dogs.

Angie: Min, thank you, are we good, Sweetheart?

Iris: Yeah, we are good.

Angie: Are you liking your food?

Iris: I'm going to check in on the food… food's good.

Angie: Okay.

Please Remember to Leave a Review

Thank you so much for reading *Dogs Still Know Best*! We hope you loved it. We hope that it made you appreciate the love and heart that our dogs bring to our lives, and how even though they leave our physical world, they are never far from our side.

It would mean the world to us if you could leave an honest review on Amazon. A review is a great way to support independent authors, give us feedback and help spread the Pointer love. It will only take a few minutes and will help other readers decide to bring the book into their hearts.

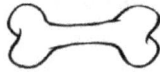

Ready for More Minnie? D.O.G., PhD is Coming!

Minnie has a lot more to say, in fact, Iris Matos and I teamed up again and spent a full year talking with Minnie. You can read more about her story in our upcoming collaboration, ***D.O.G., PhD: A Year of Conversations with a Very Smart Dog***, coming in 2020. In this third installment of the *Two Dogs' Series*, you'll have a front row seat as Iris, Minnie and I get together each month for a year to learn Minnie's perspective on life, love, family, play, work, guidance, wisdom and lessons. There are sure to be a few surprises along the way including some guest appearances, and definitely some tears and lots of laughs.

Sign up at www.twodogsbooks.com to be the first to be notified when it's released. If you're interested in being an ARC reviewer, send an email to Angie at info@twodogsbooks.com.

Don't forget to follow Minnie on Instagram: @pointtome.

Be a Part of the *Dogs Know Best* Community

Have you had any experiences after losing a beloved pet that proved that they were still with you, as an angel by your side? Have you gained insight to your pet either through an animal communicator or your own senses? We'd love to hear about it!

Follow us on Facebook at
http://facebook.com/dogsknowbest to catch up on the latest news and share your own.

About The Authors

Angie Salisbury

Angie Salisbury is an Amazon #1 bestselling author, business writer and editor and devoted dog mom. Much of her professional work includes manuals, blogs, website content, ghostwriting and other business-type writing, so her books represent a refreshing change. She is Minnie's partner and teammate in various nose work activities, and they often devote weekends to the pursuit of a new title. The two of them spend endless hours playing ball at the local dog parks until finally getting Minnie to nap time. Angie, her husband Tom and Minnie live in NE Ohio.

Iris Matos

Iris Matos, "The Puerto Rican Doctor Doolittle" is a professional Animal Communicator and Psychic Medium who shares her life with her husband, Jim and their two beautiful fur kids (Shelties), Athens and Siena. Born in Brooklyn, NY, Iris (pronounced in Spanish, "Ear-Reese") spent her childhood and young adulthood moving around to various locales, and in 2000 finally settled down in exotic Akron, Ohio. Look for her on Facebook by searching "Creating Creature Connections."

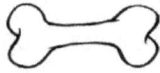

With Heartfelt Thanks: Acknowledgements

To Rev. Jenni Vinecourt, Spiritualist Reverend and Medium and the best Spiritual mentor a girl could ask for, with lots of laughs, tears and inappropriate humor mixed in. Check her out at www.revjenni.com.

To Dr. Douglas Paroff and the team at Stow Kent Animal Hospital in Kent, Ohio, for taking such wonderful care of all the Pointers and treating them as their own.

To Wendi Koontz of South Water Studios, tattoo artist and illustrator extraordinaire for the fabulous cover design. Check her out at
www.southwaterstudios.com.

To Melinda Carver for her insightful and touching Foreword to this book. Visit her at https://psychicmelinda.webs.com/.

To April Sinclair-Steinberg for her many, many years of graphic design help, not with just this project. Check our www.sinclairdesigns.com.

To Cyndee Perkins, for her insightful and impactful editing.

To Aaron Gallagher for lightning fast transcripts. His profile name is "dilsea" on Fiverr www.fiverr.com.

And to all of you readers who have followed along as I shared Bimmer and Bertram's stories, and now Minnie's, too! I can't wait to share more in D.O.G., PhD.

Also by
Angie Salisbury

Available on Amazon

The Two Dogs' Series:
Dogs Know Best: Two Dog's Training Guide For Humans (Book 1 in the Two Dogs' Series)

D.O.G., PhD: A Year of Conversations with a Very Smart Dog with Iris Matos (Book 3 in the Two Dogs' Series) **Coming in 2020**

Business:
Make Money On The Internet: How To Turn Your Website Into A Cash Making Machine with Ryan Chin

www.ingramcontent.com/pod-product-compliance
Lightning Source LLC
LaVergne TN
LVHW051045080426
835508LV00019B/1708